MW00622685

Unblinking, deeply insightful, and revealing both vulnerability and strength, Myrna Marofsky tells the story of navigating the uncertain terrain of her husband's life with dementia using love, dignity, and respect as her guideposts. Beyond being essential reading for families and care professionals alike, this book contains powerful life lessons—about adapting to all that irrevocably changes while embracing and celebrating all that endures. —**G. Allen Power, MD,** geriatrician, Schlegel Chair in Aging and Dementia Innovation at the Schlegel-UW Research Institute for Aging, author of *Dementia Beyond Disease*

A dementia diagnosis is devastating to both partners, as we witness often through CaringBridge. Myrna Marofsky's starkly honest— and beautifully loving—account of caring for her husband, Larry, through Alzheimer's will no doubt help others walking this challenging path. —**Tia Newcomer,** CEO of the nonprofit social network CaringBridge, featuring stories of hope and healing in the *Caregivers Up Close* series

There is perhaps no path more challenging than the slow, agonizing road of caring for a spouse with dementia. Myrna Marofsky has walked that road, and she has done it in a way that created a story worth telling. A love story. She is a wonderful example of the power of Unstoppable Love. —**Dan Diamond, MD,** international disaster physician, speaker, author, and coach

To the Last Dance

A Partner's Story of Living and Loving through Dementia

MYRNA MAROFSKY

WISE
INK

Time in a Bottle
Words and Music by Jim Croce
Copyright © 1971 (Renewed 1999) Time in a Bottle and Croce Publishing
All Rights Administered by BMG Rights Management (US) LLC
All Rights Reserved   Used by Permission
Reprinted by Permission of Hal Leonard LLC

Note: Some names have been changed or omitted for privacy.

ISBN 13: 978-1-63489-513-2
Library of Congress Control Number has been applied for.

Printed in the United States of America
First Printing: 2022

26 25 24 23 22   5 4 3 2 1

Cover illustration by Suyao Tian
Cover design by Patrick Maloney
Interior design by Ash Rugg

807 Broadway St. NE
Suite 46
Minneapolis, MN 55413
wiseink.com

This book is dedicated to my beloved husband of fifty-one years,
who always put a little garnish in my life.
Don't forget the parsley.

I finished writing this book during the COVID-19 pandemic of 2020.
I also dedicate this to all the people who lost loved ones during this time
and never were there to say goodbye.

"Time in a Bottle"

by Jim Croce

If I could save time in a bottle
The first thing that I'd like to do
Is to save every day
Till eternity passes away
Just to spend them with you
If I could make days last forever
If words could make wishes come true
I'd save every day like a treasure and then
Again, I would spend them with you
But there never seems to be enough time
To do the things you want to do
Once you find them
I've looked around enough to know
That you're the one I want to go
Through time with
If I had a box just for wishes
And dreams that had never come true
The box would be empty
Except for the memory
Of how they were answered by you
But there never seems to be enough time
To do the things you want to do
Once you find them
I've looked around enough to know
That you're the one I want to go
Through time with

Larry and me at my seventieth birthday event—
five years before our last dance.

Table of Contents

We Begin at the End—
A Last Dance

*I*t was the week of Halloween. Unlike past years, the house wasn't decorated with my collection of orange and black tchotchkes, witches, and carved pumpkins. There would be no little trick-or-treaters coming to the door to be greeted by Larry dressed in some disguise, acting frightened as he enthusiastically gave out candy to neighbor kids.

No, on this Halloween, one of Larry's favorite holidays, we gathered around his bed as we watched him working to breathe. He passed away the next evening.

While our last week together was filled with heart-rending events, Larry, my beloved husband of fifty-one years, gave me one final gift.

On the Monday before his death, we were eating dinner with his care aide. As usual, she was playing smooth jazz on her iPad, which made the air in the room heavy. This was her way of calming us, but for me, it was contributing to a dark and ominous mood.

"Can you find some music that is a bit more upbeat?" I asked.

She handed me her iPad. "You pick."

"Let's try some oldies."

The air around us became lighter as tunes from the past filled the room. These were our songs—tunes that Larry and I had swung to as young lovers.

Something came over me as the music touched my soul. I stood and started to move alone. Then I reached out for his hands, and while he was planted in his chair, I started swaying him to the music.

"My girl, talking about my girl," I sang. Then he looked up at me. Larry's eyes, mostly faded by this time, had a little sparkle at that moment, and then he began moving his body with me.

Larry liked what was happening as I sang, smiled, and moved crazily with him.

But that wasn't enough for me. I pulled him up from his chair to standing, and then we were swinging. He was doing what he always did when he danced—his feet were planted in one spot, while his upper body wiggled. I twirled under his arms gleefully and moved him back and forth. We were having a magical time, and my mood was lifting.

Then one of our favorite slow dance songs from years past, "In the Still of the Night," began to play. As we swayed to the familiar music, I was reminded of times long gone. I held him close, he held me, and we slowly moved in sync to the rhythm.

It was ten minutes that I will never forget.

The whole time, he looked into my eyes. We hugged tenderly. We kissed. It was just him and me. I didn't want it to end.

He gave me a last dance. It was his gift of gratitude.

Larry had lived all the days of his life.

While exhausted, drained, and full of grief, I am at peace, and so is he.

It may seem odd for me to begin my story from the end, but if there is nothing more to be taken from this book, it is this pearl: our sweet dance would never have happened if I had not kept my constant commitment to focus on love, not loss.

Dare to Live and Love

Journal entry, September 2015: I am writing a story in real time, with no idea about what the end will be.

A dementia diagnosis is devastating to *both* partners. I am one of those partners, and I know there are many like me out there.

I lost my beloved husband Larry to dementia.

Over a period of five years, I learned more than I ever wanted to know about the complexities of dementia. What began as a diagnosis of dementia due to Alzheimer's became a series of new medical diagnoses with names I had never heard before. Larry's long list of troubles first took his mind, then weakened his body, and in his final two years put an end to his ability to speak. They were debilitating and progressive. And no matter what they were called, they were all destined to take Larry's identity, his dignity, and ultimately, his life.

Dementia is a thief. It relentlessly robbed me of my husband—my best friend. Despite the imminent losses, the trick for me was not to feel robbed of my own life. I was *daring to keep living and daring to keep loving.*

For more than five years, I went through the most challenging transitions of my lifetime. Few people understood what life was like for me, a wife watching her beloved husband slowly fade away. A dementia diagnosis for a loving partner can break your heart. It almost broke mine—physically and emotionally.

This is *my* story, told from my vantage point as a spouse. It is filled with notes I made to myself in my journal, where I recorded thoughts I couldn't say out loud. There are notes to my therapist and to my family, containing recollections I can't and never want to forget. This book is designed to "get real" about an experience that is rarely talked about, or at least rarely talked about honestly. And for sure it's like nothing I'd ever heard.

It is my gift to partners faced with life-altering diagnoses, in hopes of inspiring readers to write their own stories as they design their paths to meaningful endings with the one they love. Hopefully, it will encourage a way of thinking that provides moments, hours, and even days of quality living in fragile yet treasured relationships. Through my stories and words, I hope readers won't feel alone or left alone by those who don't understand what they are going through. I get it!

There could never be a handbook on living through dementia. Everyone's experience with dementia is different. Every situation has its own complications and challenges. Not only are there wide and varied physical manifestations of the disease and timelines of cognitive decline, but personalities and tolerance levels vary. Some have limited resources. Others have different levels of support from family and friends. And still others have their own spiritual beliefs and customs that they follow.

Yet I believe there are two central questions that transcend all of these differences. These questions can guide couples writing their own stories under their own unique circumstances.

How do you want to live each day?
How do you want to feel in the end?

My answers to these questions became my compass. There was nothing more important than knowing in my heart that Larry and I had lived the best life possible until there was no more life left for him to live. While an endurance race at times, I managed to live a life with my beloved husband that ended with me having no regrets!

Dementia can't be reversed. You can't return to the way it once was. But not everything needs to be lost either.

This is the book I wish I had. That's why I started to write.

There is nothing like grieving alone to make you relive and reflect. Even though I was journaling through the experience and capturing my thoughts right after Larry died, distance and reflection did wonders, not to mention having lots of time on my hands due to the COVID-19 pandemic restrictions. I was able to dig deeper into my motivations for taking the actions that I, and those who supported me, took.

This reflection time led me to the word "gratitude." Unlike the stone-cold (pun intended), uninspiring, gray rock with the word "Gratitude" engraved on it that I once received as a gift, Larry's death allowed me to unlock a profound understanding of the word. I am grateful that I worked hard to hold on to what I could, while knowing I would be losing Larry. I never really thought about an alternative. I persevered to avoid becoming a casualty to my husband's disease, and worse yet, to avoid allowing him to become a mere shadow. That would not be a story worth writing.

Through my efforts, mistakes, and insights, there were many *aha* moments as my world turned upside down. Not only was Larry changing, but I was transforming in ways I could never have anticipated. I found a consistent message—*live lovingly through the loss, without losing yourself.* Another way of saying it is, "Don't lose your mind while they lose theirs." Not funny, but sadly, true.

This book is not prescriptive, and above all, it won't add more to the already-burdensome lists of "should dos" partners and loved ones receive after a diagnosis. I'm simply telling it as I lived it.

After Larry passed away, I had many stories to hold on to. Some were astounding, some were funny, some were heartrending. From those real-life situations, I have selected memories that provide examples of how my mindset and attitude made what seemed an unbearable situation bearable. At least "most of the time"—a disclaimer I use often. The narrative is about what I told myself and how I dealt with uncertain tomorrows. It wasn't always *what* I did, but *why* I did it.

I was urged on and supported by my daughters, their husbands, and our grandchildren. We were together, asking questions, looking for possible solutions, and living life without always thinking about loss. This made an enormous difference. And I did something I never thought I would—I began working with a therapist who offered guidance and helped me focus on the day immediately in front of me even as she prepared me for the days I dreaded most. All of this, and more, allowed me to live and love through dementia.

As I wrote, to my great surprise, stories that could have been about heartbreak and despair became a love story.

Our Backstory

Note to self: *Our love has always been about looking forward and building a future together.*

We were just kids when we met. Larry was seventeen and I was sixteen. This is hard to imagine as I look at my seventeen-year-old grandson. Both of us grew up in tightly knit Jewish communities—Larry in St. Paul, Minnesota, and me across the river in Minneapolis. For Jewish teens at that time, dating someone on the other side of the river was a big deal.

Because we were so young when we met, we fell in love as we grew up. But meeting each other as teens didn't stop Larry from asking me to marry him on our third date.

We waited until we were twenty-two before we made it official. Our love story lasted for over fifty-one years. We raised two incredible daughters, Sarah and Eve, who married the sons that Larry always wanted. And I might be biased, but our three grandsons, Max, Sam, and Nate, are the best kids ever.

Being Larry's girlfriend in college made me aware of how smart he was. He never needed to study hard because he had a photographic memory. While in law school, he typically read a case once and then could pass the test. That gave him plenty of time to hang out in the lounge playing bridge. How cruelly ironic it was that dementia would steal his memory. Although he was bright, stardom was never his goal. His dreams were simple. For me, that was perfect. He was a down-to-earth, steady guy.

We married as soon as I graduated college and got my first "real" job as an elementary school teacher. That's when Larry began law school. My salary barely paid our bills and Larry's tuition, so he had several part-time jobs. The best one was when he was a floral delivery guy. He would bring me whatever flowers dropped in the truck, mostly white lilies from large funeral arrangements. It was sweet, and so was he.

As soon as Larry passed the bar exam, he set up shop in the back room of a small storefront office with a little desk, a pen and legal pad, and one client. From there he grew his law practice that lasted forty-six years.

"Papa, what do lawyers do?" asked our grandson Nate.

"They help people solve their problems."

And that is what he did.

He was the kind of lawyer who did his work without a need for notoriety or fanfare. Yet after he died, several former clients and peers came to his funeral to honor him, and others sent me kind notes.

"Larry was a lawyer who did the right thing for the right reason," wrote one of his colleagues in a sympathy card to me.

Another client came up after the funeral and said, "In the eulogy your daughters gave, one mentioned that several of her dad's clients came after they lost a case to him and were impressed by his work. I was one of those clients. After that, I hired him, and he represented me for ten years."

The outside world saw him as a respected lawyer, but we knew he saw his main responsibility as the head of the family. That's how he was raised. It was not only a responsibility for Larry, but his source of great pride and joy.

Larry's jokes were never funny, but we laughed anyway, and as it was written in his obituary, he was a terrible singer. Because he was easygoing, rarely demanding, and usually content, he was always the guy you could rely on to be there for you and "make things feel OK." Still, he could be frustratingly stubborn, often taking his problems into his "cave," otherwise known as his head, to work on the solution himself. That's when I was seen as a "nag" if I tried to offer help. And even though he appeared stoic and passive, he was a real softie with a heart of gold. These were all traits that helped him get through the ugly years.

On the other hand, I am rarely content, with a great need to be in control. As a young teacher, I was continually looking for new ways to make light bulbs go off in the kids' minds. Even then, I was challenging the system. In my mind, there was always a better way of running the school. A pattern was emerging. When an innovative concept for a new school was proposed, I was selected to be part of the curriculum design team, which was a great outlet for my creativity.

Teaching was fun, but that career didn't last long. Hard as it is to believe, there was no maternity leave at that time, so when I got pregnant, I quit teaching, never intending to return.

Even though I was home for ten years and got to watch my daughters grow, I was restless and always dabbling in one project or another. When the girls were old enough to be left alone, I was drawn into the business world. Of course, I had no experience in business, but that didn't stop me from exploring my entrepreneurial side. Through what is called "networking" today, but at that time was called "talk to anyone you know," I met Karen, and she took me into her consulting business. I was suddenly a "management consultant," and I didn't even know what that meant. But I was good at whatever it was. A few years later, I became her partner in the business, and, as a bonus, she became my best friend.

As a consultant, I found myself traveling all over the country for days at a time, leaving Larry to manage the household when I was gone. Sarah and Eve still talk about his special spaghetti and how the local Chinese restaurant knew the standard order for "Larry" when he called. When they left for college, Larry was alone, which, as an introvert, he really enjoyed. He knew that when I was home there was always something going on.

After twenty-two years, my business was sold, and I became a consultant to women business owners who meet monthly as peer advisors. This is work I continued throughout Larry's illness and still do to this day.

People who know me would describe my personality *before* Larry got sick as restless, creative, opinionated, and above all, impatient. I say *before* because today I'm not entirely the same person I was then. Even though many of those traits served me well while Larry was sick, today, I am softer, slower, and more likely to savor moments of joy—but still impatient!

For fifty-plus years, Larry and I were like salt and pepper. It was always Myrna and Larry. Yet at the same time, we had separate identities and interests. It was a nice balance of togetherness and independence, and as a result we brought out the best in each other.

As much as we loved our beautiful home and being a tight family, Larry and I would never be described as homebodies. We were going all the time, sometimes together and sometimes in our own directions. Each of us was involved in the community, serving on public boards, working in politics, or volunteering.

While doing all of this, we watched our daughters become amazing independent women. We did the best we could as parents, despite some blips like constantly forgetting to bring Sarah flowers after her big theater productions or attending only one of Eve's tennis matches and inappropriately cheering when she hit the ball out of bounds. Family vacations through the years still provide great stories and funny home movies. But when it came to dream vacations, milestone celebrations, or our version of adventure—big cities with good food and fantastic sights—Larry and I loved being with each other. I couldn't imagine it being different.

We lived through many ups and downs, sometimes struggling, sometimes laughing, sometimes worrying, and always figuring it out together. And no matter what we were going through, as long as we could hold hands, or touch our feet under the covers, we were good.

How quickly a beautiful life can be turned upside down! Our wedding vows—*till death do us part*—were about to be put to the test.

From

Denial

to

Acceptance

No More Excuses

Note to self: *There is a quote on my computer that I continually look at. Dr. Brulov, in the movie* Spellbound, *said, "My dear girl, you cannot keep bumping your head against reality and saying it's not there."*

I saw the signs. Larry couldn't remember little things nor some important ones. He repeated questions that were just answered, couldn't perform familiar tasks, and kept buying bottles of ketchup when I sent him to the store for other items. In social gatherings he was quieter, and at home he was withdrawn.

Even two years before his diagnosis, the signs were right in front of my eyes, but I looked away, too frightened to let myself admit what I was seeing. I covered up his missteps with excuses to spare myself from accepting the truth. The "cover-up" is well known by anyone who suspects their partner has dementia, especially in the beginning when there are more normal times than symptomatic ones.

To keep from letting myself believe what I knew was true, I came up with seemingly rational answers as to why he asked the same thing over and over.

If he was confused, maybe I hadn't been clear.

If he forgot something, I told him, "You were probably distracted by . . ."

If one reason didn't make sense, there was always another "reasonable" explanation to replace it.

Margaret Heffernan, author of *Willful Blindness: Why We Ignore the Obvious at Our Peril,* calls these excuses our "alibis," choices we make, sometimes consciously but mostly not, to remain removed from situations where "we could know, and should know, but don't want to know because it makes us feel better not to know."

I knew.

As it became more apparent that Larry was losing his grip on so many things, the lightweight cover-ups quickly turned into me believing there was a perfectly good reason for his cognitive changes—he was depressed. Why wouldn't he be? His treasured daughter was diagnosed with breast cancer and beginning treatment. And to make matters even more onerous, his sweet grandson was dealing with anxiety and depression. These were problems he couldn't fix. There was nothing he could do but watch, which must have tormented him. In my mind, this was enough to cause Larry to be distracted and forgetful.

I was in avoidance and denial.

Finally, we got to the point where I was losing my patience and rather than brushing off his behavior, I got frustrated and—I'm embarrassed to admit—short-tempered, even commanding, "Get to a doctor!"

Instead of a diagnosis of depression, his doctor set him up for further testing. Little did I realize that this four-hour neuropsychological test would change our life. It took four months for us to get the results. The doctor who could interpret the results was "unavailable," and I didn't care. It was four months that I could avoid thinking about what I didn't want to know.

We never talked about the test or the pending results. My guess is that Larry filed it away somewhere in his mind. It was his way of compartmentalizing things, a trait that served him well as an attorney.

We learned our fate on a cold and dreary January day, fitting for the occasion. While we sat nervously in the lobby of the neurology clinic, Larry's name was called. My stomach dropped. To steady myself, I took Larry's hand, and we followed the receptionist into the doctor's office. Then we waited, making small talk, which neither of us cared about.

It seemed like forever until the doctor knocked on the door and entered. I couldn't read her face.

"Hello folks, I'm Dr. Anonymous. I'll be providing your test results. What a winter we have had! Do you live around here? Hope the drive wasn't too bad."

She was trying to relax us.

Larry only gave her a cryptic response. "We are fine."

This was one of the few times I just sat quietly, unable to make myself add anything. Nothing could have relaxed me.

Setting her papers aside, she looked at Larry and began asking about his history—not his medical history, but his life history.

"I see you are an attorney. How long have you been practicing? Do you still enjoy it?"

Larry nodded yes.

"Tell me about your family. Do your daughters live nearby?"

Again, he nodded his head. It was clear he wasn't willing to chat.

She kept trying. "What things do you like to do?"

We had never met her before, but to her credit, she tried to understand how the news she was about to deliver would land on a young-looking, seventy-year-old couple.

Choosing her words carefully, she slowly went through each section of the test results, which meant nothing to me. Then came the final blow as she declared, "The test results indicate a diagnosis of dementia in the form of early-stage Alzheimer's."

It truly was an "oh shit" moment, but I probably said, "Oh no!"

No more excuses.

Hearing the words "dementia" and "Alzheimer's" was more painful than I could have predicted. They were words that were totally off our radar. They weren't in either of our families, nor were we curious about them. In fact, when Larry would talk about Alzheimer's in any way, he would mispronounce it so terribly that it became a joke.

It wasn't that Larry and I had never talked about the possibility of some cognitive issue, but we thought if that was the case, it could be treated by swallowing a pill, and then life would go on. We were still young. We had dreams of growing old together with big retirement plans. In our minds, dementia was for old people.

The gravity of the diagnosis didn't hit us right away. Sitting with the doctor, trying to absorb the news, I remember grabbing Larry's arm to cling to him.

Before we could catch our breath, the doctor asked, "What are you going to do now?"

Was she really expecting us to answer that?

From that point forward, "What are you going to do now?" became a question doctors asked us over and over. We would get bad news, and in what seemed like a matter of minutes, we were supposed to make decisions.

"I want to keep working," Larry said with conviction.

Her tone changed now. "If you do," she responded, making the limits clear, "you will need someone to review all of your work and keep your schedule. If not, you will need a plan B for a new way of living."

A plan B? We'd never lived with a reliable plan A. This was our future delivered in a twenty-minute appointment.

Larry wasn't about to be under a microscope for his work. We already had several conversations about referring cases requiring litigation to colleagues so he could lighten his load by focusing on transactional work. Giving it all up would be a major decision.

If he gave up his practice, what would he do?

No hobbies and only one or two good buddies wasn't going to be enough, nor was his favorite pastime of sitting and reading a James Patterson book for hours. His entire identity was being an attorney and a wonderful husband and father.

My mind, and I'm sure Larry's, was filled with questions that no medical doctor could help us answer.

We left the doctor's office with a handful of pamphlets, a recommendation to follow up in a year, and a prescription for commonly used medications Aricept and Namenda. We had the pills we hoped would cure Larry's problems, and even though I was diligent about making sure he took them daily, I never felt they did anything.

It was now up to me to keep bad news from becoming a bad life.

Now What?

Note to self: What exactly are the "golden years"?

When we returned home from hearing a diagnosis that had just knocked us over, we both went right to our favorite spot on the sofa. Hugging tightly in the warm glow of the sun, we cried, not sobbing tears, but tears of disappointment combined with fear of the unknown.

Now what? was all I could ask over and over again in my head.

I'm pretty sure what Larry was thinking about was his future.

Since we were both problem solvers, it didn't take long before the action planning began in earnest. I started the conversation with a litany of emotional questions.

"How are you feeling about what you heard? What do we do now? How will we go on?"

As usual, Larry took a practical approach. If he was feeling emotions, he didn't show them. "I'll have to close the practice."

Struck by his statement, I pushed him. "Retire? Are you sure?"

With tears in his eyes, he simply said, "It's time."

One of the hardest decisions we thought we would ever face was made in an hour, followed by the creation of a timeline for closing the law practice Larry had built over forty-six years. It would take five months to close all the files, notify his clients, and sell his office condo. Larry's identity as a practicing lawyer would be gone by summer.

We had a solid action plan on paper. In our hearts, we knew it was a life-changer.

Giving up his practice and not having the professional designation of attorney-at-law was a bigger hit for Larry than his diagnosis. He was experiencing a punishing loss. Regrettably, I didn't realize the depth of it. I wish I would have been more understanding. "Attorney Larry" was how he was known by his clients. People counted on him.

Still sitting together, as close as we could get, we started talking about what we would do to fill our time—time we never had before. It was probably the typical retirement conversation most couples have, except ours had a big cloud over it.

"We could take the road trips we always planned but never had the time to take. We've wanted to do all the national parks," I said without conviction.

Larry didn't say anything.

I kept going, "We'd need a bigger car for travel, probably an SUV."

The conversation ended with the beginnings of a plan I was making because Larry was simply agreeing, and not at all engaged. But I was feeling more hopeful.

Within weeks of that conversation, we bought a bigger car for travel. We went to the AAA store and purchased books about national parks, travel gear, and a necessity for any road trip—a wastebasket for the car. We were ready to take off. In the end, we never took a road trip. It was just dreaming. We were *pretending* that nothing would change and avoiding *preparing* for what would inevitably change.

Hours after we returned from hearing the diagnosis, Sarah and Eve, along with their husbands, Aaron and Lawrence, were in our living room. The thought of telling our daughters was agonizing. Even though they knew their dad wasn't quite right, this conversation would be tough. In the middle of the room sat Larry on what had become known as the "famous red couch." Not only was it the most comfortable seat in the house, but it was also the place where happy and sad conversations took place. This was where we sat when I told Larry about Sarah's breast cancer, and it was also the place where we'd learned we were going to become grandparents. From

Larry's diagnosis on, it became the seat of difficult conversations.

The room was quiet at first, almost as if we were in mourning. No matter how they said the words "Everything will be OK," words they learned from me over the years, there was dread all around. Still, everyone was committed to making the very best of the situation. We were all in it together, even though we didn't have a clue what that meant.

Soon a social worker friend showed up. She worked in the field of dementia and wanted to help. I was numb with no idea what to be thinking about. I remember feeling like I was there, but not there.

As our family sat in the living room, dazed and distracted, she consoled us with kind words and shared our sadness. But it didn't take long for her to move from a family friend to her professional role as adviser and provider of The List. Suddenly, I had "to-do's."

"You will need to get your wills and power of attorney documents in order. There are tax documents you should talk to your estate planner about. You can save some money."

I thought about writing down what she was saying, but I couldn't move to get a pad and paper.

Not realizing how she was burdening me, she said as Larry listened, "Oh, and you should think about an agreement with Larry to figure out when he will give up the keys to the car. I have a contract you both should sign so when the time comes, he will see that he agreed to it."

That landed with a thud.

"I'd recommend you contact the Alzheimer's Association; they are a great resource. They can help you explore some great day programs. Oh, and you might want to talk to your rabbi for spiritual consultation."

Yikes! All this and it had only been a few hours since we learned of our new life path.

Her list was heavy and filled with head stuff, totally lacking any emotion. All I had to do was complete the tasks, and I could check them off the list. And then what? Was everything supposed to be OK after that?

I received the information but didn't pay much attention to most of it. Nothing felt right to me. Not only was I not ready to hear this, but I didn't want to. My life had to become more than checking things off a list.

Meanwhile, our hearts were aching. It's the unknowns, the emotions, and anticipated losses that paralyze a family at a time like this. I wanted to tend to everyone's heart while mine was breaking. And there, in the midst of all of this, sat Larry, listening but not talking. What must he have been thinking?

Of course, I needed to take action, but Larry was an attorney, and we had our affairs in order. Years before any of this, I prepared the "red file folder," which contained important documents like our wills and health directives. In hindsight, I wish we would have spoken to an estate or elder law attorney years in advance. It may have helped financially, and I'd recommend this to others.

The reality is that neither of us really thought about getting old and sick, let alone Alzheimer's or the possibility of dying.

There is a Yiddish saying, "We plan, and God laughs." As I've gotten older, I've learned the truth in this statement, and with Larry's diagnosis, even more so. I was facing an entirely new set of realities that were going to require me to adjust and adapt—and I had no idea how to do that. It wasn't going to be easy.

We Need to Tell Our Stories

Note to self: Sometimes it seems like Larry is considered a specimen.

*L*arry is not like the others. The doctors must have been wrong. Larry must have rushed the test, just like he did in college. He could do better. I started believing that there must be another issue that was overlooked. No, he couldn't have Alzheimer's.

In my attempt to reverse the first diagnosis, we went to another clinic for a second opinion.

This time they didn't give the big four-hour test, but the more typical one—spell "world" backward, draw a clock, count backward from forty-nine by multiples of seven. I could administer the test today to myself, but I'm too afraid I wouldn't pass. I already know how anxious I get when I'm asked to remember three words at my yearly exam.

Once again, Larry demonstrated traits of dementia. The second doctor concurred with the first—early stages of Alzheimer's. His manner of delivery was even more matter-of-fact and aloof than the first doctor's. At this point, all I had was information, medical terms, and a lot of pamphlets—no reassuring thoughts.

Then came the distressing event that started me on a quest to find my own way through what was ahead.

It was two weeks after we received the second opinion when the clinic's memory team called me. They asked for a family meeting. Thinking it was a smart thing to do, I set the date and informed our family.

Everyone showed up early with high expectations of having their questions answered and getting support for the unknown world we were facing. The receptionist led us into a sterile room where we were seated around a large conference table. Larry was by my side. Across from us were new faces—a social worker and an occupational therapist. At the head of the table was a neurologist we had never met.

The doctor took charge, immediately launching into his "doctor speak."

"As you already know, the symptoms of Alzheimer's worsen over time. We typically see three general stages: early, middle, and late. Sometimes in the early stages, patients will wander off or . . ."

As he droned on, I told myself this was not going to be Larry.

"Then in the later stages we typically see physical changes that involve grooming, dressing, ability to use the toilet . . ." He delivered his words as if he were reading an owner's manual for a new car.

"It's possible," he continued, "for some people to continue independently in the early stages. In later stages, they may require more intensive caregiving."

His final point was, "The average person lives four to eight years."

At that, I felt like I was being taken down a dark hole. I sarcastically thought to myself, *Thank you very much!*

Larry was not "some person" or the "statistically average person." The doctor was describing a situation that could have been anyone's. There was no acknowledgment of the faces sitting before him, nor was there any recognition of the sadness that filled the air in the room. Oddly, there were moments when the doctor seemed confused or couldn't remember a term. I started to think *he* was dementing. Think of it: a memory care doctor treating patients while losing his own mind.

He finished his part of the meeting with, "The next time you come, you will be seeing another doctor from the clinic. I will be retiring in a month." I had no problem with that. I already knew there would be no next meeting for us.

As each team member spoke, things got worse. I listened to their generic descriptions of what could go wrong and nothing about what could go right, even with some adjustments.

"Here is what you should prepare for . . ."

"Typically, people lose their . . ."

They painted a bleak picture of the progression of dementia. The memory team was doing their job, which meant following long-held practices. They focused on *what is*—how many beans were in the jar. Using observed patterns of how functionality decreases as the disease progresses, they walked us through the stages of what to expect. They were talking about textbook examples, not us.

We had facts about dementia—many we didn't need to know at that moment, just weeks after the diagnosis. What we didn't get was helpful guidance. I remember my daughter Sarah, seated at the end of the table at this family meeting, wearing her "cancer hat" due to her chemo treatments.

She asked the doctor, "How will we know when it's not safe for Dad to drive the boys anymore?"

"You will just know."

It was an empty and useless answer.

As the meeting continued, the social worker informed us of what she called "the necessary arrangements." As she rattled things off, I visualized a checklist in her mind that she had gone over with others hundreds of times before. She was very emphatic about the contract that Larry was supposed to sign agreeing when he would stop driving. We had already heard about this. We never did it, and luckily, we never needed it.

Then she provided what she believed to be her most important piece of advice for me.

"Join a support group. It will be very helpful as things get more difficult."

While probably a good thing for some, it was nothing I would even consider. How would she know? She never took a minute to find out anything about me. If she had, she might have realized that this wasn't an option for me. She had no idea that I always ended up leading any group I was in, even if it wasn't my job. I was also concerned that I'd hear people's stories and try to help them instead of helping myself. No support groups for me.

I listened politely but felt annoyed. We left the meeting with more books and pamphlets to take home and review, which I knew was unlikely to happen any time soon. This meeting was not an isolated case. In fact, this has become a pattern others have identified. Why? Because, as reported in a research paper written in the *AMA Journal of Ethics*, "professionals and those who support people living with dementia are grounded in a 'tragedy discourse,' which emphasizes the loss of both ability and identity, and that this view directly harms people living with dementia above and beyond the effects of the pathology of the disease."

There was no doubt in my mind that the professionals we selected were highly qualified and very smart. They knew the science. It's not that they were uncaring; however, I question what happened to a profession that was supposed to serve human beings who were suffering. It's hard to think of a family, having just received a fretful diagnosis, not needing some consolation, especially when they were sitting around the table talking about their husband and father with him in front of them.

After feeling disheartened by this meeting, I thought about what I was missing, and I realized they weren't saying what I needed to hear. And to make it worse, I didn't know what I needed at the time—but they could have. I had no preparation for the days ahead of me.

Even the most knowledgeable professionals never knew how much they let me down.

Hindsight has helped me articulate what would have made that experience, and many others to come, valuable. To start with, it would have been nice to receive some empathy as human beings who were suffering not from physical pain, but emotional pain. I wanted our unique situation to be acknowledged, and to have my fears addressed.

What if instead of a command to join a support group I would have heard, "This can be a very scary time. There is a lot to deal with and many unknowns ahead. Some people find it helpful to be in a group where stories and concerns can be shared with people in a similar situation." It wouldn't have changed my thinking but would have been received as more caring.

What if Sarah's question about her dad driving the boys would have been answered with, "I'm sorry, I can't give you an answer. Everyone is different. I'm sure your dad has enjoyed being there for your sons and helping you out. It is one of those things that is hard to face. All I can say is, you will see the changes and then you will know."

I wanted Larry to be seen as more than a man with dementia, but as a person—an accomplished attorney, a great husband and father, a man whose fear of the diagnosis was made so much worse by hearing it said aloud.

Then it would seem appropriate to include me in the equation. I wanted to be seen as his wife who was in the beginning stages of grief and who was now very confused—a partner who suddenly was responsible for maintaining a caring relationship with her husband. And how great it would have been for our family, too young to have spent any time thinking they would be losing a parent to such a dreadful disease, to receive some consideration. Learning about the characteristics and progression of dementia was important, but I wanted more. How could they be helpful if they didn't know anything about us? All it would have taken was for them to learn something about Larry, me, and our life.

That meeting would have been very different if they gave us even a hint of hope. There was no suggestion that we could still have a few "good" years without life being completely altered. What if they talked about possibilities of years when simple supervision and monitoring, along with some adaptations, would be all that we needed? And even when explaining the more ominous side of dementia, what if they talked about preserving the things that would enable us to maintain some qualities of the life we once had? How calming it would have been to receive encouragement that we could still see flowers bloom and watch sunsets together.

Hope was not part of this conversation. Dark days seemed imminent. As a result, everything felt urgent and discouraging.

The meeting with the memory team became the impetus for writing this book.

Unless people like me are honest and start telling our stories in ways that others will really hear them, these conversations won't change. Facts aren't enough; they have no meaning without stories. It's all the variables in each person's story that will transform how we talk about dementia and ultimately how we thrive and survive through this heartbreak.

Let's talk about the experience of losing a beloved partner to dementia and its disruption of a life lived. Let's talk about the importance of our relationships and the emotional loss we experience amidst all the other losses. Let's remind others that there can be good years before the difficult ones, or at least good periods of time in the midst of the hard ones. And let's support our loved ones by talking openly about their loss of autonomy and their ability to determine the way they can live their lives.

Hopefully as professionals hear our stories and understand them, they will eliminate the frightening tragedy talk. When the people we turn to as experts understand the human side of dementia, they will be able to provide guidance that will actually be helpful.

Once we make apparent the benefits of this affirming discourse, perhaps insurance companies will allow doctors to take the time needed to listen to the stories being told to them. Maybe psychologists can be included in more useful ways than just testing.

It is well known that women comprise 63 percent of unpaid caregivers in this country. Many are wives and partners. Like me, they bear the burdens and physical loads on the other side of the disease while at the same time hurting emotionally from losing the one they love. Who cares for the caregivers?

I was left to find my own way.

Crazy as it sounds, I'm actually grateful for the meeting I just described. It fortified my commitment to fight like hell to keep despair away. I would attempt whatever could be done to preserve some "normalcy" in our life. Somehow, I would figure it out, but it would take courage and strength to stay the course.

It was only when Larry was at his worst and I had come to the end of my five-year mission to understand Larry's unusual constellation of diagnoses that I finally found a remarkable doctor who put things in perspective for me.

This final appointment ended my search to find answers.

All it took was a soft-spoken, empathetic neurologist to say, "Larry has such a complex situation, it should be written as an article in a medical journal."

Oddly this felt reassuring. "Doctor," I asked, "what are the chances of someone getting this diagnosis?"

He turned to his computer, did a few calculations, and swung around to look at us.

"One in eighty thousand cases."

Taken aback by this statement, I turned to Larry and said with irony, "Lucky us."

Then in a most compassionate manner, the doctor spoke the words I needed to hear, "Yes, but think of the eighty thousand things you are grateful for over this lifetime."

Beautiful!

As he got up to leave the room, his parting words for me were, "Take care and be kind to yourself."

Oh, how I wish I would have received this message in the beginning!

There Is No Cure—
Yet

Mayo Clinic Headline: "Alzheimer's treatments: What's on the horizon?"

"Despite many promising leads, new treatments for Alzheimer's are slow to emerge."

J couldn't make myself say Alzheimer's. Whenever I'd have to describe Larry's condition, I'd freeze and then say quietly, "He has early-stage dementia." I was stuck in denial, and, while I can't explain it, somehow saying dementia didn't seem as bad. After all, Alzheimer's is dementia. It's also something that seemed far too frightful a condition to accept for Larry. Whenever I could avoid saying anything, that's what I did.

As much as I tried to deny or minimize Larry's diagnosis, I couldn't.

Yet anytime there was a headline that even remotely referred to some breakthrough in Alzheimer's, I was all over it. I'd try anything if I thought it was a cure, or at least a treatment. I chased down a clinical trial that used an insulin nasal spray as a possible treatment, only to be denied access. When I showed Larry's internist a study I found about the possibilities of increased insulin dosage as a way to improve cognition for Alzheimer's patients, he agreed to a small increase. Following many months of giving Larry insulin injections, there was little change.

One evening the nightly news caught my attention with a featured story about the positive results of marijuana use as a treatment for Alzheimer's. I had heard this before but discounted it as just another theory. But it stuck in my head, so I did some research, even reviewed some scholarly articles, and found enough confirming evidence to make me want to try it. But I was never a flower child, nor had I been exposed to recreational drugs, so I had no idea how or where to get marijuana. All I had to do was ask around, and I was amazed to find out how many people had a source. That's how I found little heart-shaped, marijuana-infused chocolates. Heart-shaped seemed appropriate for a wife to feed her husband. Each night I fed Larry a small piece of the chocolate. Then I took an equal "dose" for me.

Feeling pretty smug about our newest treatment, I wanted to let Eve and Lawrence know that their ancient mother was cool.

"I have something I want to tell you," I said as we sat in their backyard.

Eve got scared. "Oh no! What?"

I nervously confessed to her about our nightly chocolate escapes.

"That's it?" she said, and then laughed so hard I felt stupid.

I guess my revelation was much ado about nothing for a younger generation.

While a novel experiment, I saw no positive results for Larry after almost a year. But for me, a little chocolate each night helped me relax, and sometimes a little more helped me sleep well.

Sadly, for a person who believes there is always an option, I could find no convincing way to treat Alzheimer's.

The last statistic I read was that one in fourteen people over the age of sixty-five will receive a diagnosis of some form of dementia. Billions of dollars have gone into research on Alzheimer's, with no significant findings, not to mention any cures. Occasionally, a headline will pop up claiming an experimental drug is showing promise, or a treatment has been released, even if it is surrounded by controversy. And still, after years of research, most big drug companies have ended their work, concluding they don't want to invest more in a treatment when the cause is still uncertain. All these trials and studies have resulted in more questions than answers.

I'm not trying to be a downer, but the facts speak for themselves—no cures and no answers, at least for the near future.

There was no escaping it. We were facing an incurable, life-altering disease, and I was scared.

Knowing this and feeling frightened wasn't helped by the portrayal of dementia in the media and in books. They all told emotional stories of people's challenges from the disease or family hardships of living with someone who has dementia. As the population ages, there are more and more dementia stories in movies and on TV. I try to avoid them because they are painful, and I know how they will end.

But there was one movie that I saw just a few years before Larry's diagnosis that sticks with me to this day. It was a foreign film called *Amour.* In that movie, we see a devoted older couple where the wife has some form of dementia. As she declines, her husband gives up everything to keep his promise to her that he would never let her go to the hospital. He lovingly cares for her, feeds her, and reads to her until she can no longer get out of bed or take nourishment. With nothing more for him to do but watch her suffer, he puts her out of her misery. With love in his eyes, he takes the pillow and suffocates her. Months later, they show him at peace. After watching the ugliness of this seemingly compassionate act, I left the theater emotionally drained and conflicted. Had he done a cruel thing or an act of loving kindness? There were days when memories of this movie haunted me.

Better than hanging my hopes on a pill that might become available in the future, my only choice was to design a life that accepted Larry's dementia, but at the same time did not make him an invalid. I had to live *with it,* not manage it.

A

Wedding Vow—

Devotion

I Am Larry's Wife

Excerpts from the speech Larry gave to me at my seventieth birthday party: "Having you accept my proposal was the happiest day of my life. After all these years, through all we have gone through, nothing has changed. You are the one and only for me."

Larry, one hour later: "When is it time for me to give my speech?"

Shortly after Larry's diagnosis, I had a meeting with a social worker from the clinic we were using. I was anxious and had many questions. In her attempt to provide assistance and advice, she felt it important to give me her recommendation.

"You need to get Larry on a list for a memory care facility now."

I looked at her and thought, *Are you kidding?*

She was serious and continued, "The facilities have long waiting lists. You want to make sure he gets in and has time to adjust to a new surrounding before his condition worsens."

My negative reaction went unnoticed because without a pause she continued, "Sell your home and find an apartment near Larry, so it will be convenient to see him daily. I can give you some names of facilities."

I remember how angry I was when I heard this. Not only was she assuming the worst, even suggesting an urgency, she had no consideration of our loving partnership as husband and wife.

A decision like the one she suggested would have destroyed us.

I was Larry's bride. I knew him better than anyone—even with his dementia.

Not only did we love each other, but we loved being married. And, true to a long relationship, there were times that were happily normal, and then there were times that were incredibly hard. The aftermath of Larry's diagnosis was one of those very hard times.

I would always be Larry's loving wife, but with dementia now part of our life, that role took on a new meaning with new responsibilities and challenges. Things had to change.

As my husband, Larry always believed he was my protector. After he got sick, I became his protector. That wasn't easy for him to accept. For me, the switch became increasingly difficult as I watched him disappear before my eyes. I couldn't help but see all the things I was losing, while failing to see what I still had. It was solitary, scary, and overwhelming. I didn't want to lose anything, but I believed I had to find a way not to lose everything.

The loving relationship we had built was being threatened by not knowing how long we would have together. Jim Croce's song "Time in a Bottle" was correct; there was no way I could make days last forever.

While my responsibilities to him changed, I could never see myself as my husband's caregiver. It felt exhausting to think of having a full-time job of giving care because it implied I would totally dedicate myself to Larry's disease. I didn't want our last years together to be filled with doing things *for* him instead of *with* him. Besides, I had never seen myself in any role related to nursing or caregiving. Just ask my daughters. If they were sick, they went to "Dr. Larry." Caregiving wasn't in my DNA—or so I thought. I wasn't his caregiver, and he wasn't my patient. Larry needed to feel like I was his partner and he was mine—husband and wife.

Still, I felt like I had to have a way to let people know I was Larry's advocate when explaining my situation to others, so I kept trying to find a term I could accept. I used "care partner" at times. It seemed to embrace the notion of working together in the midst of an illness. But the only thing that felt comfortable was to say, "I am Larry's wife." That's who I was and would always be.

It didn't take long for me to learn that it was difficult for others to really understand what it was like for me—a wife living beside her loving partner with dementia—unless they were in a similar situation.

It wasn't only social workers telling me to sell my house. I soon found that friends and acquaintances didn't know what to say to comfort me. They would make well-intended comments that didn't help.

"It was really hard when my grandmother had Alzheimer's . . ."

"I had an aunt who ended up . . ."

They couldn't comprehend the enormity of having my reality changed forever. And sometimes their lack of understanding made me want to yell, "But you don't understand, this is my husband, who I have lived with and loved for most of my life." But I never did.

In a reflective moment, as we were approaching the first anniversary of Larry's death, my daughter Eve said, "Mom, it had to be different for you. This was your life partner. You had the daily grind together, and we went home."

She was right. Larry and I shared ordinary things for fifty-plus years. But this was an extraordinary time. Our life together and our lives separately would never be the same. It was surreal.

For two people who were together for more years than we were apart, Larry's diagnosis presented a life we had never envisioned. Decisions were now mine. Finances were totally my responsibility. The little secrets or shared memories between us became mine to keep. I couldn't say, "Do you remember when?" without disappointment. It was frustrating to ask, "What do you think about . . . ?" And while we tried to stay intimate, it just wasn't the same.

While it seems obvious, I want to state loudly: if you are the loving partner of someone with dementia, as I was, you are in the midst of the trauma as well.

There is no escaping that fact. As Larry's wife, I was living dementia very differently than he was, but still living it twenty-four hours a day. Without his full presence in my life, I felt incomplete. Larry and I had built a solid life together. We could never have imagined things would be any different. But they were. My foundation was crumbling.

This was my new reality. I had to find a way to determine the right path for me.

In the beginning, my brain spun with no focus because everything felt urgent, and my mind was all over the place. I couldn't normalize things because I had no idea what to expect. That's why I kept questioning myself and others, believing if I asked the right questions, I could find my way. I didn't always find answers, and sometimes when I did, I didn't like what I found. And then there were times when no answer was the right answer.

It was only after I adopted a belief in possibilities and took actions that, in many cases, defied commonly held predictions of *what's to be* and instead focused on *how it can be* that I found hope in our situation. It was more uplifting than anything I had heard from others.

What I discovered was that these possibilities didn't come from learning more information about dementia as a disease. I saw possibilities when I leaned into the way Larry and I had always lived our lives, the things that were important to us and even, at times, some of the more modest dreams we shared. I knew what I had to do because we were already doing it.

For five years as Larry's wife, I was shaping a reality where we could keep living and loving, rather than just coping. It wasn't always easy and there were times when I felt defeated. This may sound bold, but I am convinced that focusing on the husband-and-wife relationship with Larry enhanced the quality of the time we had left together. And an even bolder statement is that it slowed his cognitive loss, keeping his brain active and maintaining his ability to function independently—all delaying his decline and sustaining his personhood.

Of course, I knew I couldn't control the terrible progressive conditions that had taken over Larry's mind, but I believed I was capable of managing my mind. This attitude and mindset led me to actions that gave us a meaningful life together. I had air to breathe at times when I struggled with knowing I was losing my husband and best friend.

Surrender Wasn't an Option

Note to self: I hate hearing that demoralizing description of dementia as "the long goodbye." I prefer the words I received from friends: "Life is tough, my darling, but so are you."

A good friend and I were catching up on life sometime after Larry died. She knew both of us very well and spent a lot of time with us over the years. As we chatted, I spoke about this book, which piqued her interest. Her own husband was exhibiting some cognition issues, so it was on her mind. In the course of the conversation, I shared my underlying theme.

"I worked hard not to give in to Larry's disease."

"What do you mean by not giving in?"

I thought it would have been obvious, especially to her, since she had a family history of dementia, and she was with Larry and me so often. But it wasn't, and this became an *aha* moment for me. I realized I did have a different way of looking at dementia.

"I wasn't going to be constantly thinking about the effects of dementia, Larry's limited abilities, his physical needs, or what he couldn't do."

She still looked puzzled. "But he had dementia."

"Yes, I know, and it was hard for me to accept that, but if I gave in to the disease, I would be treating Larry like an invalid. I didn't want to see him as frail, and—just as important—I didn't want him to feel like he was sick."

She persisted. "Well, he never looked sick, but he wasn't the same guy."

"He still had feelings and knowledge of what was happening. He still loved to go and do. Think about the Dylan concert we all went to a few years ago. It had some difficult moments, but we did it. If I forgot that Larry was still very much alive, we would have had no quality of life together. All I would see was what we were losing, instead of embracing what we could still have and how we could live *with* dementia. Giving in would have been surrendering our life to dementia."

Then she understood. "It's like giving up."

It's not easy to fight a battle you know you are going to lose. Yet I knew if every day I felt like I was confronting the enemy of dementia, I would eventually *give in,* which would mean giving up. I chose to *give to* our relationship because that was the only real option for me. Here is the difference:

GIVING IN	*vs.*	**GIVING TO**

He is dying.	*He is very much alive.*
My life as I knew it is over.	*Things will change, but there is still much living ahead.*
He can't.	*He can, with some adjustments.*
He will never know.	*He still has feelings.*
Doctors are right.	*Doctors are trying.*
Poor me.	*There still are beautiful moments.*
I can't.	*I still can.*
I need to give up my . . .	*I need to keep active with things that bring me joy.*
I'm afraid.	*I'm sad.*
They are in charge.	*I am in charge.*

It was several months after Larry's diagnosis before we established a style of living that was mostly doable, somewhat satisfying, and an alternate reality we both were beginning to accept. Then things started to get harder, and I grew anxious and uncertain as to whether I was fighting the right battles. Reluctantly, I attended a day-long workshop organized by the Alzheimer's Association. The mere fact that I was willing to go meant I needed something, but I had my doubts that this was it.

Within minutes of walking into the large convention center, filled with several hundred people, I began questioning why I had agreed to come. I told myself, *These are not my people,* and I actually felt embarrassed to be in this crowd. I couldn't accept that I was one of them.

Instead of asking myself what I could learn, my head kept saying there was nothing for me there. Usually I'm a meet-and-greet person, but that day, I tried to hide. I knew I had to get over it, so I went back to the challenge I gave myself whenever I attended conferences in my consulting days—try to find one thing to take away, and you will feel it was worth attending.

Since I had already questioned whether I belonged, I chose not to follow the regular track of workshops. Instead, I attended the workshops designated for professionals, which proved to be a great choice.

That was when I discovered Dr. G. Allen Power, MD, an international educator on transformational models of care for older adults, particularly those living with cognitive issues. Listening to his presentation was like listening to the Dalai Lama. He reinforced what I believed. Dr. Power spoke of caring for people with dementia as a human rights issue. He said we blame everything on dementia and focus on what the patient can't do or might not be able to do, instead of asking, "What are the chances that things could go right? What's the risk of not doing something?" He spoke of the choice of words we use, like "doing *with* you" versus "doing *to* you." I could go on and on about what I got from that session, but suffice it to say, the impact was powerful. I walked away reinforced in my beliefs about how I wanted my life to proceed. I couldn't and wouldn't surrender to dementia.

Larry needed to keep his sense of self, despite his illness. For him, it meant being seen and being acknowledged for what he is, what he was, and what he could still be, even with dementia.

I knew I had to become Larry's champion, his advocate, and sometimes his cheerleader. That shift didn't come easily. As he became more and more dependent on me to guide him, these roles were even more important, forcing me to play them as best I could.

Some days I didn't feel tough enough to fight, but I tried—words I say repeatedly. They are indicative of what my life was like—hoping to live the way I desired for as long as possible. Was it an audacious hope to defy predictions and do it my way? Perhaps, but with some help I found my path.

I needed to become intentional about keeping Larry as my partner in life rather than a patient to care for. Giving to, not giving in, and for sure not giving up.

What

about

Me?

I Wasn't OK

Note to self: I'm probably walking around looking like Eeyore with lipstick—gloomy and gray.

It was just a few months after Larry's diagnosis, and I thought I was doing OK. I was reluctantly coming to terms with Larry's dementia, being a loving wife, attending to the family, and trying to establish a lifestyle that worked. But in reality, decisions were becoming difficult. Larry's dementia presented too much uncertainty, and I was struggling. Some mornings, I couldn't face the day ahead of me, let alone think about the days to come. Sometimes, I'd let myself sob in the shower, so Larry couldn't see.

Embarrassed to admit my weakness, I kept everything to myself, never admitting to anyone my fears or confusion. Above all, it was important to me that I never looked pathetic—to anyone. As would be expected, this resulted in sleepless nights and elevated blood pressure.

I wasn't OK. I had become a different person and it was noticeable. I could tell that my irritability was impacting the way I interacted with Larry. My patience was limited and my tolerance was low. I'm sure he felt it. I could see him retreating to his chair to avoid upsetting me.

The extrovert in me was longing to talk to someone. But to whom? Larry was no longer my support system, and I didn't want to reveal my innermost thoughts to my daughters. It was nothing my sister or dear friends would understand—they were already feeling sorry for me.

I finally admitted I needed outside help.

That led me on an unexpectedly strange search to find a therapist I could talk to.

The first therapy encounter came a few months after Larry closed his office. I selected a person paid for by my insurance who had an office close to our home—not the best criteria. I really didn't know better since the only therapy I had experienced was physical therapy, which is quite different.

Larry came with me since I was convinced that he had the problem, not me. My goal was for the therapist to help *him* learn how to retire. He had nothing to do, and that is exactly what he did—nothing. I believed that if he kept busy, both of us would be happier.

After waiting for a few minutes in the lobby, a very short woman with frizzy gray hair and giant glasses came out to meet us. She made a quick introduction and led us to her office. Then she commanded us to sit on her sofa as she climbed into her big chair across from us. Her feet didn't reach the ground so she swung her legs as she spoke. All I could think of was Lily Tomlin's character Edith Ann sitting in a giant chair.

The mismatch between the serious reason for our visit, the proportion of the therapist to her chair, and the impersonal feeling I had distracted me. I couldn't concentrate. Still, I wanted to be open to her advice.

She began, "Why are you here?"

This question caught me off guard. We had just settled in our seats. There was no chatter, no small talk, and no questions to get some background. I thought this was a bit abrupt, but again, therapy was new to me.

Charging ahead, I provided her with an abbreviated summary of our family's troubles over the past years, Larry's diagnosis, and the stress we were living. Then I answered her question of why we were there.

"Larry needs help finding his way in retirement. He is bored."

She snapped her head and glared at Larry. "Is that true? Are you bored?"

"If she says so."

I thought the therapy part was actually beginning when she continued, "Larry, what do you like to do?"

He didn't seem to want to answer, so I jumped to help. "He likes to play bridge."

She addressed Larry sternly. "If you like bridge, why aren't you playing?"

He gave her a cold stare and, in his lawyer tone, responded, "You need four people to play bridge."

We weren't getting anywhere.

After forty minutes she looked at me and pointedly advised me to relax more. "Try meditation," she said as she showed me two meditation apps on her phone.

The session ended with her recommending I come back alone next time. I didn't return.

Things didn't get much better with subsequent attempts.

I arrived early for my next appointment and was greeted by a golden retriever who immediately began to drool on my thigh. Then the therapist came out and told me the dog was part of her therapy. Since I wasn't about to have a dog for a therapist, I politely and promptly left.

Up next was a therapist who was in the midst of a personal crisis and talked about her own issues. I couldn't help but provide her with coaching. It's just what I do, and it kept me from talking about myself. But I was paying by the hour. After two sessions like this, I felt like she got more than I did. She was out.

The fourth attempt was by far the worst. It was the final straw and put a halt to looking for a therapist.

This time I went with a recommendation from people at the memory clinic. I had high hopes. As I was parking my car, I saw a sign that said "Hoarders Association" on the front of the building. Was I in the wrong place? Inside, there was literature all over about hoarding. Apparently, hoarders were the primary clientele for this clinic with a few patients from the memory clinic thrown in.

The office was cold and barren, which was probably right for hoarders, but it wasn't working for me. The therapist began our session by informing me of the payment procedures. Never asking any probing questions, she spent most of the time advising me to think about how I could change my life. Her advice didn't match my value system. She was out.

All of this and it was just the first year living with Larry's diagnosis. After these experiences, I had no interest in pursuing therapy.

Get Help!

Note to self: I feel like I'm pushing a giant rock up a hill. When it slides down even the slightest, I'm disappointed— it's always a setback.

J came undone in Napa, California.

The work I do is to run peer advisory groups of successful women business owners. A group that I had been leading for twelve years planned their annual retreat in the wine country of Napa, California. As their leader, my job was to facilitate the meeting. Many of the women planned to bring their spouses.

What could be lovelier than Napa in the spring?

I decided to take Larry along, thinking he could read by the pool while I attended meetings. It seemed perfect. He could go for walks and meet us for meals and some of the activities. I was apprehensive but not too worried. I even added two extra days to the trip to spend in our favorite city of San Francisco. I don't know what I was thinking. It was a mere fantasy.

The retreat was held at a beautiful hotel resort with views of vineyards on a hillside across from the outdoor deck. It was a warm breezy evening. The flowers seemed especially fragrant and noticeable since it was still cool in Minnesota. I started thinking this was going to be a respite from the worries at home.

We began the event with a happy hour beside the pool. Spouses who were with their partners attended, including Larry.

What started out as a lovely evening quickly became stressful.

Most of the women in our group knew Larry as a friendly, lighthearted guy. That night, he was quiet and withdrawn. Drinks in hand, we chatted, and as they tried to engage Larry in conversation, I could feel my stomach churn, praying he would respond if asked a question. My mind was in two places. I was trying to be a good leader of the group, but at the same time, I was worrying about my husband who was unpredictable and obviously not his old self. It wasn't a "happy hour" for me.

During the day, as the women met, Larry sat outside reading. I'd check on him a few times at a break and sit with him at dinner. One afternoon, spouses were invited to participate with everyone in a pizza-making contest.

The leader broke everyone into small groups. Larry was with three women he didn't know. I was assigned to another group but always watching to see how Larry was doing. I could see that his team members recognized he had a problem, but they tried to involve him as much as they could. He seemed fine, allowing me to participate enough to make a delicious pizza and win the contest. All was good.

The next morning as I prepared for the meeting, I glanced out the window and saw Larry walk past. Was he going for a walk? Was he looking for breakfast? I was totally distracted, but knew I had to turn to my job.

Susan was the first one in the room. I'd known Susan for over ten years. As she started talking to me about something she was dealing with, she quickly recognized that I wasn't listening to her.

"Myrna, is everything all right?"

I didn't answer.

"What's going on? Something isn't right."

Unconvincingly, I said, "I'm fine."

At this point the other women were taking their seats around the table. But Susan persisted loud enough for all to hear.

"Is Larry OK? He doesn't seem like himself."

I didn't answer her right away because I couldn't make up anything that would sound true except the truth. And then out came, "No, nothing is OK!"

The rest of the words rushed out. There I was standing at the end of a long conference table, in front of fifteen women, confessing. I was raw, I was ragged, and I was real. And it felt horrible and great at the same time.

It was obvious that the women had participated in private conversations about our situation. When it finally came out, these caring, kind women surrounded me with love. They let me talk. I'm sure I blathered, yet they listened. I told them about Larry's diagnosis and my struggles as I dealt with it. I wanted to assure them that, as their leader, I would not let them down. I would be there no matter what. My thoughts were disjointed but out there. I remember trying so hard not to cry, and then it was impossible to stop. We had to pass the box of tissues around the table for all of our tears. Many had known me for years and were aware of the stress I had experienced from previous medical nightmares in my family. Their compassion and concern were undeniable.

I received their empathy and felt their kindness, but I'm not sure they understood the disappointment I constantly faced, like right at that moment in Napa, a trip that was supposed to be glorious.

It was a very difficult encounter, and yet one for which I will always be grateful. These were strong, bright women. They were leaders used to directing and then being followed. With heartfelt words, they made me promise to get help.

They were right. I knew it. So I agreed, already knowing it wasn't going to be easy. They didn't know about my failed ventures down the therapy route. Yet as unusual as my first four attempts at therapy were, they taught me a lot. I came to realize that I was part of the problem. I wasn't looking in the right places because I wasn't being honest with myself. Life was going to be difficult. I had to change my thinking. I knew I was needy, but I hated that I really didn't know what I needed. I had to find someone who did.

I made a promise to the women in Napa that night, and they were going to hold me accountable.

I Was in the Right Room

Note to my new therapist: I see this therapy as me being vulnerable and you being insightful.

Her response: This is a beautiful way to talk about what good psychotherapy is—how it should work, its purpose. I could not agree more!

After my experience in California, I came home and spent the entire next day searching the web for a therapist. I was convinced someone was out there for me. Searching Google, I landed on the *Psychology Today* referral site. I read and reread the bios of anyone who triggered a response. I went to websites and read everything they had to say. Of course, I wanted knowledge and relevant experiences. More importantly, I looked for tone, for something that told me they would understand and work collaboratively with me. I didn't want someone to give me another list of hard things to do or more things to manage.

If I really wanted guidance, I had to let myself be vulnerable, which meant I had to find a therapist who would create a space that allowed me to do that. I had to feel comfortable in the discomfort of pouring my heart out. Dr. Brené Brown, a noted author and speaker, describes vulnerability as that unstable feeling we get when we step out of our comfort zone. She debunks the myth that vulnerability is a sign of weakness. She would say finding someone to whom I could expose my emotional turmoil was a sign of courage.

I needed a therapist who had knowledge of how to guide me. But what I really wanted was a person who connected to my heart.

That day of searching the web is still crystal clear in my mind because of one listing I found—a licensed psychologist. What stood out and differentiated her from others were her words that combined empathy with knowledge, and understanding with whispers of hope. I felt like she was speaking to me.

After a short phone chat, we set up a meeting.

Right from the start, I could tell she was smart yet not intimidating. But the selling point was that at the first appointment, she demonstrated that she understood me. She understood that dementia is more than just memory loss and losing things. Never assuming that she knew what my life was like, she asked different questions than I'd been asked before. After a short conversation, I knew she would be my partner in what was to become a relationship that lasted for four and a half years until Larry's death and through my first years without him.

Thanks to the women in Napa, I was finally in the right room. I found a safe place for hard conversations where I would learn about the gift of therapy at a time I needed it most.

I had always believed it was up to me to take care of myself. With Larry's condition, I didn't know how until I found someone who could help me live without dread and act in hope.

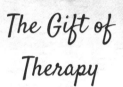

The Gift of Therapy

Note to therapist: Please let me stay in la-la land as long as possible, but don't sugarcoat what I need to know.

My first therapy session began with these words: "While my priority is to live lovingly with Larry, I need help getting through this without losing myself or dying too."

I learned from my failed therapy that it was critical to state my desired goal right from the beginning and admit out loud that I didn't know how to achieve it.

There was no time to waste. I needed knowledge-able guidance that would keep me alive. I needed help figuring out how I could retain the important elements of my life that I cherished. Of course, my marriage was at the top of the list, but I also wanted to keep working, being Nana to my grandkids, and having a social life, while knowing Larry's dementia would be a factor in all of that.

I started serious therapy for me, and I was ready to own it. It was not an easy process, given my stubborn nature of resisting asking for help or being perceived as selfish, and of course never looking pathetic.

At the end of that first session, to my surprise, I received a diagnosis of PTSD. I thought Larry was the one with an issue that had a name. Apparently with all the heavy lifting of the past few years—family issues on top of Larry's diagnosis—my mental health was at risk. There was a lot to do. I spent every Wednesday afternoon on the "therapy couch." Weekly, I'd engage in conversations aimed at problem-solving and designing creative options to manage the spheres of my life. Weekly, my mental health was nourished. Weekly, my therapist approached our work with two questions that became my most valued principles. *How do I want to live each day? How do I want to feel in the end?*

As I told my story and shared my concerns with my new therapist, I immediately felt a sense of relief. I was talking and she was listening—really listening. It didn't take long before I expressed my worries about my daughters. They were consuming my mind too.

"I worry about my relationship with Sarah and Eve. I need their support as I move through dementia with their dad, but I don't know how much burden I can put on them."

Her response came without hesitation. "They are in this right with you. Can you get them here so they can be part of the conversation?"

"Tonight? We just got started!"

"Why not? It's important that they understand our going-forward thinking from the beginning."

We wasted no time. The girls and I returned three hours later.

Bringing my daughters into the conversation early was the right thing to do. The first thing my therapist did was make it clear to them that I was her client and that they were there to learn about our process so they could support me. They left the meeting understanding that I would keep fighting the impact of their dad's dementia as much as I could and for as long as it made sense. Understanding that each of us would have our own experiences and perspectives on the situation, we were all on board.

My A-team was assembled. I had the right therapist, someone who knew nothing about me or Larry, allowing me to be vulnerable and not feel judged. I had my daughters. Even though they had limited knowledge of the private moments Larry and I shared, I knew they would be there every step of the way. And then there was me, unsure of what was to come, but open to receiving support as I stepped into the unknown.

Hesitantly at first, I began to unwrap this gift of therapy. My therapist and I were in this fight together, knowing we would stop only when it was obvious that we had to transition and get ready for Larry's end. I give few recommendations in this book, but one that I feel important to make is to find someone, if not a professional, then a trusted friend or loving sibling, to walk by your side and lean on when you are weary and confused. As you live your dementia story, having someone who will listen with empathy and kindness is essential. This is too hard a journey to walk alone. Sadly, with a dementia diagnosis, you are often walking alone even with your partner physically by your side.

In our early sessions, we spent time talking about reinforcing existing patterns of behavior that Larry could follow easily. We determined how to establish new patterns that could prevent scrambling later. It was a form of triage. I was encouraged to observe and then talk with Larry about our daily and weekly routines. Then I was to report back in the next session. We would use that information to figure out how to preserve patterns of behavior and the cadence of our lives. We talked about engaging the location services on both of our phones and using the navigation programs in our cars while he was still driving. Yeah! Something I could do that didn't require deep thinking.

I was doing things meant to keep Larry's sense of himself and his autonomy. The benefit to me was that everything he could still do—with small changes in preparation—meant something I did not have to take over or manage. My therapy sessions taught me that the question was not can he, but under what conditions could he do something he had previously done?

I was developing a strategy that fit my wish of living and loving through dementia. I was also learning about myself and realizing there were patterns I needed to break, mostly around my interactions with Larry.

A good example of this came about four months after I started therapy.

We were at home when Larry came near and said, "It's lunch time."

That meant he was expecting me to stop what I was doing and make a sandwich for him.

I snapped, "Make it yourself. You've made the same turkey and cheese sandwich for all the years you were alone in your office. You can make it now!" I must have been having one of those days.

Troubled by this experience, I asked my therapist, "Was I cruel for insisting that he make his own lunch? Was I a bitch?"

From the look on her face, I could tell I was about to get a lesson. "Larry had an established pattern—he made his own lunch for years. You need to strengthen that pattern by letting him do what he was familiar with." Then with a little smirk, she suggested I make another change. "Encourage him to make his own lunch. Just leave out the sarcasm next time."

A big part of my early learning was to assess a situation before judging or criticizing and if possible, help him, not rescue him, or worse, make him feel bad.

It still was early. I was being prepared for harder things and didn't realize it.

With each situation I'd bring to therapy, we would review my observations and consider what could be possible. Then in real time we would determine the next steps. If we thought Larry was confused or frustrated, it became an opportunity to do something different or accommodate and adjust. We couldn't stop Larry's cognitive and functional loss, but we could prevent or minimize loss that didn't need to happen.

Several times over the years, I would come to sessions with some version of, "I've been thinking about selling the house and looking around for a one-floor townhouse. If I'm ever going to do it, I should do it now so Larry can get used to it."

At times like this my therapist would ask me with a knowing look, "If you do that, will you gain more than you risk losing? He knows where the light switches are."

It was her way of saying that he knew his way around our house. Why change things that could create a larger problem?

She was right. Larry was proud of the home we lived in for almost forty years. It was his domain where he felt content. He had his patterns—get the paper, take the garbage out, feed the birds. I wouldn't want him to lose his independence by leaving the home he loved. It would be a setback for not just him, but both of us. I wasn't really serious about selling the house. I didn't want that. Just thinking about leaving our family home was emotional, not to mention it would be another huge loss for me. I had enough grief to deal with. It was one of those easy fixes, a flight response, for my much bigger fears.

That was a good reminder for me: stay with the patterns that can help remind each of us who we are.

I understand that our decision to stay put might not work for everyone. We could still handle the big house, the stairs, and the home maintenance. It was our safe haven of love and comfort. Keeping Larry at home remained one of my most important goals. It was important to both of us.

Many unknowns about Larry's condition consumed me, and—even knowing there were no answers—I'd wonder out loud in my therapy sessions, "Why did Larry do that? How was he feeling? What was he thinking? How was he experiencing life?" I knew these were not real questions, but fleeting thoughts driven by curiosity, but it always felt good to ask them anyway.

Then, using her eloquent words along with her professorial knowledge, my therapist would provide her explanation of what was happening in Larry's brain and mind. Usually this would become a vivid metaphor.

"It's like he is looking into a fisheye mirror and sees a distorted image. Some edges are blurred or out of sight and some are in full view."

I visualized it as she spoke.

"All of this gives confusing reflections of what or who he is looking at. Some may think that's a fun experience, but in reality, it is frightening."

That was a powerful metaphor. I got it! Well, almost.

There were times when I'd ask unanswerable questions, "What do you think is going to happen next? What should I be ready for?" Then I'd wonder if I really wanted to know.

That's when she would try to calm my anxiety by saying, "I can see some things that are coming—things you may not be ready to hear."

These words landed like some cryptic omen psychologists would share. They felt strange, almost like something a psychic once told me—followed by her advice to spin like a Sufi whirling dervish to release my worries.

But the reality was that her words provided what I needed when I needed it. This was a real counterpoint to the bleak predictions from well-intended doctors and social workers who tried to "prepare" me when Larry was first diagnosed.

After I started writing, I finally understood how she was pushing me as much as she thought I could be pushed and allowed me to live in the moment. Through our therapy sessions I was being guided to an end that ultimately brought me to my last dance with Larry.

I'm not an easy patient. I required a lot from this skilled psychologist during those years, but she got me to see things from a more positive perspective. It was fragile hope grounded in one important word: *relationship*. I could not destroy my important relationship with Larry, for sure, but also with my family and with myself. It was the basis for everything we did together.

Selfless Not Selfish

Note to therapist: I get so caught up in "stuff" that I don't see how my sparks turn into lightning bolts and cause electricity in the house. It's shocking! (No pun intended.) I'm not sure I can ever relax and let things just flow.

Her response: I'm not sure that will happen either. We're not going to rewire you to turn you into a yoga master. But flow in your life has not relied on "relaxing" anyway. Finding your flow is going to be different.

There was no doubt in my mind that if I went down, the entire ship went down. It was evident that I set the temperature in the house. I remember my mother cautioning me about being agitated or upset around my infant daughter. When she started wailing, my mother said, "She is upset because you are. She can feel you." Well, so could Larry. In fact, I often thought he was watching to see if I got upset over something that didn't go as it typically would.

I had to stay sane.

While I totally embrace the theory and importance of mental, physical, and emotional self-care as a way of increasing dexterity, decreasing anxiety, and promoting wellness, I found I needed to address this in my own way.

I had a lot of motivation to maintain equilibrium and keep my sanity. All I had to do was look around. Many of my friends or their husbands were not well. Some were very ill, others cognitively challenged. Two of my acquaintances passed away soon after their loved one did. They lost themselves while losing their partner. Besides, I had warnings from my therapist and my daughters that I couldn't let myself be endlessly victimized by Larry's disease.

And, while I tried to deny it, I was aging myself. My body reminded me of this daily.

In a blunt yet caring conversation with Sarah, she affectionately told me, "Mom, I've already lost the dad I once knew, and I don't want to lose you too. We need you."

Dr. Jason Karlawish, author of the straightforward and revealing book called *The Problem of Alzheimer's*, writes about the broad impact of an Alzheimer's diagnosis. "It creates another patient," he says. "The caregiver, who generally forgoes their own care to give care."

Oh, how I wish I could write that I was diligent about daily meditation, practicing mindfulness, or exercising on a schedule. I can't write that.

To give myself some grace, I did work at taking care of my mental health with years of therapy. Still, it wasn't the only way to keep sane—something so easily and unintentionally ignored when a household is in turmoil. I'm fairly certain that if I hadn't attended to my own well-being, the final scenes of this book would never have played out as they did.

Knowing I needed to focus on myself as I focused on Larry, I considered where I was depleted. I started seeing several wonderful, caring wellness professionals to provide the nourishment I was missing.

My massage therapist understood emotional pain. As she put her skilled hands on me, she told me my legs were aching because my root chakra was out of whack. "That means your foundation is being torn from under you."

I saw an acupuncturist, who listened to me go on about my body aches and pains then gently said, "I think we will work on stress too."

On a particularly difficult day, she told me to scream as loud as I could. As weird as it sounded, I drove home and all the way up Highway 100 screaming and making sounds I never knew I was capable of. It was a huge release. One which I highly recommend.

Joining a wellness center that had a therapy pool provided a calming retreat. Whenever I could, I'd sneak away, get into the pool, and feel like I was being hugged by the warm water. I'd immediately relax and often meditate. Sometimes I'd find myself crying in the pool, but no one ever knew because we were already wet.

I took actions that were foreign to me, but the mental relief was evident.

When it came to what was happening to my body, that was another story. It was falling apart. The physical demands on it were becoming problematic as, over time, I was taking on more tasks as Larry became less and less mobile. No discussion about keeping sane can happen without talking about the exhaustion and irritability that pain can cause. It was made worse for me because I was stubborn and believed I was invincible. Needless to say, this attitude caused injury to my knee and exacerbated my previous back issues. Many days were made harder than they needed to be. I was crabby a lot.

The physical damage to my body only got worse as Larry started requiring more and more help getting in and out of the car, out of bed, or up from a seated position. When I tore the meniscus in my knee, I was prescribed physical therapy. The provider asked how this happened. I explained that I was caring for my husband and probably using my body wrong when assisting him. He gave me a look of sympathy and then proceeded as he would with any other person having a similar injury.

Anyone who has been to PT knows that you leave with pages of exercises to do at home. I'm sure it was good for me to be instructed to do twenty reps of this or that three times a day, but the reality was that it gave me one more thing to deal with, meaning one more layer of stress.

It was only when *I* asked a young physical therapist to teach me a better way to transport or assist Larry that I benefited from my sessions. I find it interesting that little attention, if any, is paid to teaching the partner how to prevent physical damage to themselves when, as professionals, they should know that taking care of someone who needs assistance can cause an injury. Again, where is the concern for the caregiver? My injury could have been prevented with a few preemptive words of caution and timely training.

I had to figure out how to reduce my physical load.

YouTube videos saved me. I found videos that provided proper instructions on working with someone with physical impairments. Because of the nature of Larry's situation, some didn't apply, but others gave me just enough to make transport easier.

Many of my physical problems came because I stubbornly resisted accepting the ways I could help Larry and keep from hurting myself. To be fair, I never even knew about assistive devices that could have helped us. And I'll ashamedly admit, when I did become aware, I ignored them. I didn't want them all over the house, especially when people came over. That would be a sure sign that Larry was getting worse.

It took a while for me to reexamine my thinking and have a serious conversation with myself. I couldn't get injured when I was needed the most. This was my life now. I had to stop caring about what others would think.

In reality, anyone who came into my home completely understood.

It was amazing to learn what so many already knew—grab rails, toilet bars, tub benches, and other accommodations would help me as much as him. The trick was to learn how to use these items correctly and then coach him to use them.

With this recognition, Amazon packages began coming regularly with item after item. Once I had grab bars installed in the bathrooms and at the entry stairs, Larry had something other than me to hang on to. He had a walker on each floor of the house so one was always where he was. There were bars on each side of the toilet so he could push himself up, instead of me pulling him.

I still wonder why no doctor ever recommended that we get a handicap tag for our car. It took a friend to ask me why I didn't have one. Of course, I didn't think of it because in my mind, as long as Larry and I could walk we were taking a space for someone in real trouble. Well, we were in trouble. All it took was a phone call and a doctor's signature and I had a handicap tag that allowed me to use a space when I thought it was necessary. Many days I was only willing to take Larry with me on an errand because I knew parking would be easier. But every step I took to lessen the strain on my body made life easier for me too.

I knew, without a doubt, that my body was my most important tool. I needed to speak to it in a loving way, respect it, listen to it, and take care of it so it would take care of me.

Beyond my body, my spirit was low, which had a marked effect on my motivation. Some mornings I would wake up and dread the day ahead. Despite all the activities, errands, and busyness that was going on, I was lonely. My partner was there, but not really there. My freedom to run on a whim was curtailed, and as Larry became silent, I was home and alone in solitude.

One day I heard a talk show guest speak about the effects of isolation on one's well-being. We heard a lot of this during the pandemic. The commentator's advice was to create landing points in the day and week where you routinely carry out the same activity. It could be at two in the afternoon you take a walk outside or set aside some time for reading. Wednesdays might be lunch out or Sunday nights pizza. I never was good at anything regular, but I began to set aside time to recharge, relax, and change the pace. Sundays were different than Mondays. Mornings had a pace different from afternoons. And everything moved at a slower tempo.

In this isolation, our home became even more important for my mental state. Unlike those who feel at home in any environment, it was important for me to keep some semblance of how things were. If things weren't right, I wasn't right. That's why I tried to keep our home a place that brought me comfort. Making the bed each day, plumping the throw pillows on the sofa, buying orchids to display, and keeping them blossoming became more important than ever. It was something I could control.

My attempt to follow the "get exercise" recommendation on the classic list of how to maintain sanity resulted in just the opposite.

A little over a year after Larry's first diagnosis, I signed both of us up for "buddy" personal training at the YMCA. It seemed smart at the time, but it was a mistake.

Chelsey, our trainer, really understood how to work Larry's brain while exercising. We would do boxing with gloves, going left-right-left-left-right. Good patterns to follow. Then there was the TRX straps for pull-ups. She would count our repetitions, but Larry watched me to follow what I was doing, always trying to stop before the reps were done.

Sounds good, right? But I never went to the Y by myself.

When I was with him, I had my eye on what and how he was doing. Instead of being a stress reliever, it became a stressor. If I changed machines, he followed me. If I had to go to the bathroom, he did too. Then I had to make sure to find him if he was finished before me. It was an undeniable problem that I hadn't intended. If I had to do it over again, I would have set aside a time each week for me to go to the Y alone.

Even when Larry no longer had the strength to work out, I didn't make time to use my free Silver Sneakers membership. It was a bad call on my part. It would have been a good sanity break.

At these intense moments and many others, my Apple Watch would ping, and the BREATHE icon would flash, notifying me that I wasn't taking in air. Breathing is a good thing. Many times, I would pause and do a one-minute breathing exercise, which helped a lot.

A few years ago, I attended a conference where one of the presenters demonstrated the impact that just shutting your eyes can have on your brain chemistry to calm you down. It really works. When challenges became intense, I'd shut my eyes for just a minute and sometimes more and get immediate relief. This is a practice I still do often, just not while driving.

From all of this, I realized that to stay sane, I needed to be intentional about what would keep me healthy and feeling centered. Notice I don't use the word "balanced." There is no balance in life. I discovered this long ago. Some days, months, and sadly, hours are just better than others.

It was more than therapy or the pampering self-care that helped me keep my sanity. It wasn't about taking cleansing breaths, but that does help a lot. In fact, I have to take one now to continue.

It was about giving myself permission to pay attention to my well-being at a time when Larry's illnesses could have overtaken every aspect of my life. This became a critical element in me ending this story as a whole person. Focusing on myself was not selfish or needy. It was selfless and needed!

I've now adopted a new wish for others: be kind to yourself.

Attention

with

Intention

Moments Become Memories

Note to self: What do I really want to remember about this time? I fear there will be more that I want to forget.

For years and years, Larry and I found joy making memories together. We took memorable trips, celebrated milestone events, danced at our daughters' weddings, and welcomed grandbabies, and afterward we'd say, "We will never forget."

Alzheimer's changed all of that. It was apparent that making big memories with Larry would happen less and less and, eventually disappear altogether. That's when I started collecting what I call "scrapbook moments."

As a teen, I had a scrapbook filled with dried corsages from high school dances or proms, napkins from favorite restaurants, and programs from plays and concerts. Almost all of these items were from carefree dates with Larry. They were pleasant memories but only markers of times and places.

Currently, I have over twenty thousand photos in my iPhoto library and boxes of printed photos taken before digital cameras came into play. I love taking pictures to recall fun times and to remember people and places.

These are great memories—as long as I look at them.

Scrapbook moments are different. They are snapshots of periods in time when an image, an instance of joy, or a simple event is consciously captured and brought forward later, complete with feelings and emotions. These moments often happen unexpectedly and become some of the best memories. When I recall my scrapbook moments, I am transported to them and I feel them all over again.

I needed these memories when Larry was still alive and we were struggling. They brought forward something to distract me when I longed for a pleasant thought. Now I need them even more for an occasional smile or a sentimental thought. They aren't like a photo or a dried-up corsage that I can hold in my hand. They are mental movies that I hold in my heart.

Working with my therapist, I realized that it's more than the memories that make this concept powerful; it is the process of noticing them.

I developed a watchful eye, observing beautiful, sentimental, heartfelt, funny, and anchoring moments with Larry. Then I preserved them in my heart and mind. I had to be intentional about looking for them. The more I looked, the sharper my eyesight became and the more I found. I compare it to times when I was about to buy a new car. All of a sudden, I'd start noticing cars everywhere. Cars were on my mind. I'd tune into the makes and models right down to the differences in shades of red, my favorite car color. That's how I captured scrapbook moments, even the smallest ones.

It was much easier to see the joyless side of Larry's dementia. But switching my attention to seek out moments I wanted to preserve kept some of the pain away. I was able to find comfort during chaos, and recalling these memories still brings me consolation, especially with Larry gone.

For me the best part of reliving a scrapbook moment is that the space between the event and the memory is eliminated. I can leave out the things I want to forget. It reminds me of how Mrs. Whatsit, in Madeleine L'Engle's book *A Wrinkle in Time,* uses the image of an ant walking on a flat string. The ant can get from one end of the string to the other by walking its length, but if you fold the string and bring the ends together, the ant can reach the end much more quickly and easily. In the book it's called "tessering." It is a great description of how capturing these moments can eliminate the darkness and shine light on what is worth remembering.

I love that I can bring back a scene where Larry is relishing a slice of his favorite birthday cake. It is heavy with frosting, just as he liked it. I hold the image of him carefully cutting off the frosting and saving it to eat after the cake. The frosting was the best part for him. I grin. I still feel my satisfaction knowing he enjoyed his treat, and I can forget that in his final year he would eat cake, aspirate from the crumbs, and scare the hell out of us.

There was no mention of Larry's weakened body when my son-in-law Lawrence recalled how Larry greeted him with his vice-grip handshake, squeezing with all of his might. Lawrence would fake being crushed and drop his knee to the floor. It was a game they played for all of one minute.

As Lawrence shared his memory of this scrapbook moment, he was reliving it. I could feel his connection to Larry and the fun that surrounded their special greeting. The end of Lawrence's story was sweet. He pointed to the side of his mouth and, with a twinkle in his eye, showed me how Larry's mouth would curl, ever so slightly, trying to smile. His little handshake shtick demonstrated that he was still strong, something he was always proud of. Lawrence's reaction was his way of showing love and respect. It was more than a game.

A scrapbook moment that always makes me smile was the few hours of joy I experienced about three years after Larry's diagnosis. Larry and I took our grandchildren to a Children's Theater Company performance of *Cinderella*. The show was wacky and silly. It was a good thing the stepsisters were over-the-top funny because they kept my mind on the show and not how I would handle someone needing to use the restroom.

During one of the crazy scenes, I looked over at Larry and saw him laughing really hard.

My ten-year-old grandson Nate turned to me and said, "I don't think I've ever seen Papa laugh like that."

Then his brother Sam chimed in, "Me either!"

But the memory making continued. The show's ending was a rollicking version of "Y.M.C.A." where the audience stood and joined in the movements. It was wild. I turned, and there was Larry, on his feet, arms flying in the air, trying to make the right moves with the crowd. He was into it! I would never have expected a time like this. I grabbed a quick photo, which I look at and laugh about with a full heart. But the image itself didn't capture my intense feeling of happiness as I watched Larry enjoying life. That feeling is embedded in the unforgettable memory of this incredible moment.

My most cherished scrapbook moment took place every night. It began shortly after Larry received his diagnosis. Just before we kissed and turned off the lights, I'd say to him, "Good night. I love you."

I could always count on his response. "I love you more."

Later in his illness, he'd mumble these words. In his final days, he told me with his eyes, and I'd say, "I know, you love me more."

It seemed important for him that I hear it each night. I like to think it was his way of saying, "Thank you."

I miss that exchange tremendously.

Thanks to Eve and Lawrence, I have more than scrapbook moments to hold on to and remind me of these nightly exchanges. They heard Larry say to me, "I love you more," many times, and they knew how much these words meant to me. They also knew how much I missed hearing his voice in the later years when he lost his ability to speak. For my birthday, the September before Larry passed away, they gave me an amazing gift.

It was a birthday I really didn't feel like celebrating. Things were looking dim for Larry and there wasn't much joy in my heart. I also didn't like that I was turning seventy-four. It was a big number.

Not wanting to let my birthday go unnoticed, the girls made a good attempt at doing something special. I'm sure they were struggling at that time too. They made a lovely dinner, and as usual, all of us were seated around our dining room table with Larry at his spot at the head right beside me.

The cake appeared flaming with the many candles, and everyone sang "Happy Birthday" to me. Aaron, Sarah's husband, was doing his usual silly rendition, in an attempt to lighten things up. I looked at Larry and, while he wasn't singing, his eyes were locked on my face. In my mind I could hear his monotone singing. I felt his affection. I felt his presence.

After the candles were blown out, Sarah and her family gave me cute cards with handwritten words of love.

Eve got up and ran out of the room, returning with two small packages which she handed to me. Then she and Lawrence sat back in great anticipation as I opened them. One was a rectangular box which contained a clear plastic bar. At first I didn't understand what it was.

Eve explained, "Before Dad totally lost his ability to speak, Lawrence and I recorded him saying, "I love you more."

We had talked about recording Larry speaking but never did—or at least I never did.

"We turned his words and voice into sound waves and had them printed on acrylic," Eve continued.

I looked at the colorful waves on the thick, ten-inch bar I was holding, and I immediately burst into tears. I could never have dreamt of anything like this, and I was incredibly moved by their thoughtfulness. I kept looking at it and couldn't put it down.

Then I opened the smaller box. It contained an iPod with a pair of earbuds. On it were additional recordings of words I had heard Larry say hundreds of times but had been missing terribly. I had his loving words!

Sarah yelled to Eve, "OK, you win for the best gift ever!"

Receiving this gift was an amazing scrapbook moment. The bar of soundwaves sits on my nightstand. I glance at it when I go to bed. Not only do I see it, but I can hear him. He loved me more.

Scrapbook moments served a dual purpose for me. They were collected memories that I tucked away to call upon when I needed a bright spot in a day or when I was overtaken by grief, but the process of discovering them kept me from looking in the rearview mirror and thinking about a past that was no more. I was tuned into appreciating life's special moments—moments that could have easily been missed.

The hundreds of photos and videos that I have remain beautiful remembrances. But there is something even more special about my treasure trove of delightful scrapbook moments. While they are recollections of Larry, they also provide reflections of my role in making many of these memories happen. They remind me that with intention I could find things to be grateful for, even in our difficult times.

I have souvenirs!

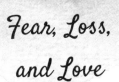

Fear, Loss, and Love

Note to self: Despair is inescapable at times. I keep looking at Larry and thinking, "Where did you go?" I've come to realize how alone I am and how many of him there might be.

While I was getting more and more discouraged with the rapid and constant change we were experiencing, I could see that Larry was aware of his losses, too, and it was literally killing him. He was sad and frightened in ways I could only imagine. His autonomy was at stake. His life was being cut short. While unspoken, I believe he felt the emotional toll of loss to his last days. He was scared, really scared.

After being by Larry's side for so many years, I realized that in his mind he believed he had failed me. He could no longer be the man he once was. It made sense. Here was a man of strength and intelligence, my go-to guy for everything. In our house, you could hear me calling from the top of the steps to him on the bottom, "Lar" this or "Lar" that. And now he was losing all of that. Meanwhile, he watched me getting stronger, leading others, paying the bills, working with handymen instead of him. I had to assist him with everything, including, to his horror, helping him with his toileting. I continue to feel bad that I hadn't realized the terror he felt.

One shattering episode that revealed his fear and totally blindsided me happened when my therapist and Larry met at a session less than a year after his diagnosis. She wanted to get to know him, and since I was seeing her so often, I wanted him to know her.

As we sat side by side on her sofa, it was evident that he was nervous and uncomfortable. Trying to build rapport with Larry, she asked a series of light questions, but all she got back were one-word answers. Then she dug deeper, asking about his fears after the diagnosis. To my surprise, he admitted to her that he was afraid.

That's when she asked, "What are you afraid of?"

Without hesitation and with certainty, Larry proclaimed words that shocked me. I can still feel the sting. "She might leave me."

I flinched and turned to look at him. He wasn't looking at me, but at her.

She kept calm and probed, "What do you mean leave you?"

"I think she will divorce me."

In disbelief, I sat quietly.

"Do you think she will leave you for good? Do you think she would leave you alone?"

"Yes."

Yikes! I was mortified. Who was this man sitting next to me? I couldn't comprehend how he didn't see that I was totally committed to him. I would never leave. How could he say such a thing?

I was totally bewildered and mad. I don't remember anything that was said after that. The air had been sucked out of the room and words didn't matter.

It was a long ride home.

Over and over in my mind, I struggled to determine where things had gone wrong. Was our love story over? I was very close to giving up, and we were just in the first year of dementia. If I accepted that this was how it would be, then I believed all I could do was suffer through it. My life would become an endurance test.

I was able to debrief this disturbing session with my therapist a couple of days later. After spending a lot of time talking about my anger, sadness, and embarrassment, we shifted to Larry. We talked about how somewhere in his mind he believed he would be left by himself in his terrible condition. It was likely he recognized his failings and believed he was disappointing me to the point where I would leave him.

Trying to get into the mind of someone with dementia is not easy, but we both believed that some deep emotion was driving him, and it wasn't me. With a lot of discussion, we came to the conclusion that his statement about me leaving came from his tremendous fear of being alone.

Some lingering experience from his past may have triggered this fear, and because I was always by his side, because he knew he needed me as his rock, because he was feeling helpless and hopeless, his focus turned to me. He couldn't express his anxiety, and out of his mouth came the distressing statement that I would divorce him. The psychological explanation for this was way too deep for me. All I knew was that I was hurt, and he was hurting.

No matter what the reasoning was, I couldn't stop thinking about the emotional torment he was experiencing yet could not articulate. I had to make myself believe that he didn't have words other than "divorce" to express himself. He didn't mean to be cruel.

I began to assure him repeatedly that I was right by his side, using lots of loving words and tender hugs. Every day I tried to give Larry a heartfelt compliment, but it needed to be intentional because there were hard days when kind words didn't come easily. And at the risk of sounding pitiful, I would have liked some tenderness myself.

As hard as this conversation with Larry was, it probably changed me forever. The impact went way beyond the event itself and became one of the biggest *aha* moments of my life.

Once I really felt his fear of losing *me*, I faced my own incredible fear of losing *him*. It was a pivotal moment.

I was so involved in fighting to hang on, dealing with daily "stuff," and fretting about the little things, that I never allowed myself to face my real fear. He would leave me, and I would be left alone—without him. It took understanding his apprehension to face my own. That was one of those sad times when I let myself cry.

How strange it was that this awakening made me realize that Larry was "my beloved," a phrase I had difficulty using before. Whenever my therapist would refer to Larry as "my beloved," I would squirm in my seat. It felt like something from a Hallmark card. Of course, I loved Larry. I knew he loved me. In fact, he idolized me, sometimes to the point of feeling like he wasn't good enough. But over fifty-plus years of going from young love, to love with distractions of work and family, to fights that made us doubt our love, to mature love where we needed each other more than ever, I never thought about the questions from *Fiddler on the Roof.* Tevye, bewildered, asks Golde, "Do you love me?" and Golde, who has grown accustomed to her role and relationship without ever giving conscious thought to love, questions back, "Do I love you?"

This story is short but the realization that came from it was powerful. It's a good thing it happened early in our journey through dementia because it allowed me to reframe my thinking. We were both frightened that we would lose each other. Despite the harshness of his words that I would leave him, I had an awareness I wouldn't have had before. Once I understood his fears, I had to bravely face my own. And, without a doubt, I had to make sure Larry knew that I was never going to leave him. Bearing with the emotional toll of dementia required courage.

As I was writing about this, a strong memory popped into my head. It was of a trip to Israel that Larry and I took together in those "good old days." One day shopping the streets of Jerusalem, we stopped in a jewelry store where we gazed at two matching gold rings. We tried them on and agreed that we would purchase them and each of us would wear the same ring. Cut into the gold of the ring was the sentiment from the Psalm "The Song of Songs," written in Hebrew. Translated it says, *I am my beloved's, and my beloved is mine.* We wore our rings for many years as a symbol of our love.

Larry's words were powerful reminders that love cannot be taken for granted. Separately and together, the words "my" and "beloved" had an intensity I hadn't felt before. Our love was the reason I was committed to fight so hard.

Mirror, Mirror on the Wall

Note to self: I need to determine how we are going to live. It's a challenge to do this and not become a lesser version of myself.

My mother rarely spoke about the frustrations in her life. For this reason, a rare exchange between us sticks with me. Like me, my mother never wanted to be seen as weak or helpless, and for most of her life she was strong and independent. But there were times she felt out of control and mad at the world. If you were around her, you knew she was upset, and if we didn't recognize it, she let us know. These episodes never lasted long because she had a technique to reset herself. It's something she shared with me many times.

"I'd get up," she explained, "look into the mirror, and say, 'Clara, get yourself together. You are strong. You know what you need to do. So do it!'"

And she did.

There were many days I felt like my mother—days I couldn't make sense out of my life. I had days I wasn't sure what to do or couldn't make a decision. And some of those days I actually looked into the mirror to talk to myself.

Myrna, accept that there is no miracle to be found. Find a direction that feels right for you and Larry. You know you can figure it out. So do it!

Looking in the mirror also prompted me to put on some makeup to help me feel alive. Lipstick and blusher do wonders.

I really didn't need a mirror. When I sat across from Larry, looked into his eyes, and saw the way he looked at me, I was aware of what he was thinking. I knew what to do. We had done hard things together for more than fifty years. His illness would continually present challenges and life changes, but Larry and I lived by a set of values about life and how to live it. Our values didn't need to change.

I found my internal compass by asking myself two questions: "How do I want to live each day?" and "How do I want to feel at the end?"

My aching heart knew the answers. In the end, I wanted to feel satisfaction, knowing that I had done everything I could. Larry would always know that I was by his side. He would be treated with dignity and respect. I wanted him to know that I loved him forever. And in the end, I wanted to feel whole, even with a hole in my heart without him.

Once I was able to answer these essential questions, a set of guiding principles emerged and informed my beliefs and actions. I never realized this happened at the time, but I always felt like something was guiding me, enabling me to feel a little bit more confident as I took one step after the other. I would lean into these principles because they felt like the right way to think and the right things to do. They were a part of me and a reflection of the relationship Larry and I had together and constantly asking myself, "What would Larry want?"

There was no checklist or printed list anywhere until now.

See Larry as a complete person. He is more than dementia.

Help Larry keep his sense of self and identity.

Keep Larry in the action, include him, go with him, have fun with him.

Remember that Larry still can make decisions, especially about his life.

Keep Larry at home, unless you have no other options. (This is a decision I will never, ever, regret.)

Keep your traditions and patterns, then build on them. They are as important to the family as they are to Larry.

Ground yourself in hope and always be on the lookout for it. It will lead to possibilities.

Keep talking, even when it's a monologue.

Protect your identity and hang on to your own sense of self. It will help you be a better companion to Larry.

Be honest with Larry and yourself.

HUG LARRY A LOT!

Living with these principles allowed me to have short periods of relaxation, because I didn't have to think very hard about what to do, I just did them. And with Larry always in the action, we still had fun times.

Of course, there were days when I was caught off guard because I wasn't tuned into his changing abilities. I could unexpectedly have the wind knocked out of me, assuming nothing had changed. I desperately wanted to hang on to the image of Larry as I knew him, but things had become too difficult for him, and sometimes I forgot that.

When he couldn't change a light bulb in a ceiling fixture—something he had done many times—I kept pushing him.

"Try it this way."

"Turn it a little to the left."

He tried but just couldn't figure out how to get the cover off, keep track of small screws, and balance the glass fixture. Plus, he was on a ladder with me holding him by his belt. Not a good scene, for sure!

When I asked, "Do you need help?" I made it worse because I was calling out his inability to do a simple task. He gave me a look of defeat and shame.

Finally, I realized he just could not do it, at least for that morning. It was too much. We had to stop trying.

I'm not sure what happened, except that I handled the situation all wrong. I hadn't considered what might have become too difficult and allowed him to give up with dignity. I veered from my principles because I really wanted to see Larry as the guy who fixed everything. It was one of those days when something little tipped me into wishful thinking.

Getting used to making decisions alone when they were about our married life was new to me, and there were always decisions to be made. Some were easy, but when I had to make difficult decisions, especially as time went on, my guiding principles helped me think through my choices. Notice I said, "think through them." Sometimes my soul-searching created more questions than answers. Usually because there was no right answer. Should I listen to a urologist's recommendation about surgery? We did and we shouldn't have. Is it time to bring in a lift chair? We did when it was really needed. How important is it to visit his brother in Florida? We did, it was hard, and it was the right thing to do. And to be totally honest, sometimes I had to trust my gut and answer, "What do I want?"

I never sat my daughters down and said, "Look, we are going to live by this list of guiding principles." They naturally understood them, even if I had to remind them of why we were doing things at times. We kept our Friday Shabbat tradition because that's what we always did. If Larry did something odd or unusual, they never laughed at him. And when he deliberately did something he thought was funny, the girls delighted him with a laugh and the familiar, "Oh Dad!" Dignity and respect were what Larry deserved and what he got.

And something very important to me was that we didn't trick Larry or lie to him, and I never saw any family member marginalize him even when he wasn't able to think clearly. I'm always offended when I hear relatives of people living with dementia say the insulting statement, "He won't know anyway."

That's why this story told by two nurses who work with dementia patients in their homes stood out to me when I heard it.

An Alzheimer's patient they were caring for was having difficulty giving up driving. He loved to drive his car and could not remember that he had agreed with his doctors, his wife, and his kids to stop driving. As long as he could find the keys, he would go to the garage, start the car, and drive off. First, his wife thought it might work to hide the keys. But he managed to find the keys again and again. Frustrated, his wife sought the advice of the nurses. She figured they had seen this kind of circumstance before and may have some ideas. The nurses were concerned that it was not just the man's safety at risk but also the safety of others in his community.

Putting their heads together, the woman and the nurses devised a plan that did prevent the man from driving. They reasoned that if it was not working to hide the keys maybe the key itself needed to be disabled. The wife went to the local dealer, explained the situation, and came home with a blank key—something that would fit in the ignition but could not start the car. They replaced the working key with the blank key. It didn't stop the gentleman from getting the keys, taking them to the car, opening the garage door, and attempting to drive away. That sequence unfolded just as it had for some time. But he was no longer able to start the car. Confused, he questioned his wife, who told him the car needed repair. The man became frustrated, even angry. His reactions seemed inevitable, but the problem was solved. He was no longer endangering himself or others.

I'm sure the nurses' story is missing a lot. We don't know anything about the man's conditions, the couple's backstory, or the frustration the wife was feeling. But what I reacted to when I heard it was the use of deception to solve the problem.

If he was well enough to find the hidden keys, it would seem reasonable to think that he might have known his wife and visiting nurses may have tricked him. I can only think the husband felt demoted as a human being.

The entire scene left me with many questions about intentions and guiding principles.

Could he trust his wife any longer? She certainly knew she was tricking him, and if it worked this time, why wouldn't she use deception again?

What was guiding the wife? Did she see him as an aging man with dementia who was a threat to the safety of others? A burden to deal with? Did she see him as her partner? Would this deception and the power dynamic impact the relationship for the time they had left together? Why were safety issues the only concern? Did they consider his autonomy or self-respect? And why did these nurses think this was a good example of addressing one of the hardest losses for their patient?

Certainly, there were times when sticking to my principles was inconvenient or burdensome. But unlike the story of the nurses, I tried to stay away from deception and manipulative fixes that might solve a problem in the short term. I had to think long term, continually asking myself, "How do I want to feel in the end?" When I looked in the mirror, I had to reflect the person I was and always wanted to be.

Finding

Normal

Patterns, Routines, and Traditions

Comment to Larry: The kids are going to Hawaii. Would you like to go back to Hawaii?
Larry: I'd go anywhere with you.
Me: You'd go with me to Hell?
Larry: We are already there.

Amazingly, in the first two years, Larry's decline appeared to be slowing. Was it all the activity, his feeling of self-worth because he was helping me around the house, or just how his disease was progressing? I will never know. What I do know is that the establishment of patterns—routine tasks he knew and predictable activities—was working. The tension surrounding us seemed to have lightened because I was finally accepting reality enough to do what made things better for both of us.

This was a time when I really understood the importance of looking for existing patterns of behaviors in Larry's life, then reinforcing them so he could repeat them. This was great because he didn't have to process information in order to perform. Knowing what to do and when to do it made things easier for me and calming for him. He also retained these patterns later when it got harder to teach him new things.

As long as I didn't change things or give him more than one thing to do at a time, we did OK. No, it wasn't Larry who needed to change, it was me. I had to give up on my casual, last-minute ideas and adjust to a new pace.

Every day I had to think of things Larry already knew how to do, could still do, and might want to do. Then I'd make a list for him to follow. This was a suggestion I read about in those pamphlets and books the social workers gave me. Except our list wasn't in an ordinary spiral notebook. That would have been too easy. Without really thinking about it, I started the process in a very particular style of notebook. It was an executive looking 5″ × 7″ size, with lined paper and a sturdy black cover. Not only was this a special notebook, but I had to write everything using a thick black felt-tip pen, with the day noted on the top of each page, and—most importantly—it required a checkbox next to each item. If it wasn't in this format, Larry didn't take it seriously. Referring to his list often, Larry would go about his day and check items off as they were completed. The little love note I occasionally wrote at the end seemed to go unnoticed.

If I left him home alone for any period of time, the list had to include reminders such as "play solitaire on your iPad." If we were going to do something together, like an appointment or lunch with friends, it was on the list.

This notebook became his anchor that oriented him for the day. The patterns he followed allowed him to keep doing what he was familiar with and not think about what he could no longer do.

It also provided a reference for him other than me, even though I'd have to remind him occasionally to check the list when he looked to me for guidance. Beyond the notebook, Larry had his routines—tasks he had done for years. Sunday, his job was to change the bedding. Thursday, the trash cans needed to be put out. Every day he prepared the same breakfast. I miss the wonderful smell of his English muffins in the toaster.

When he was still driving, he could still run one errand at a time.

We had a routine that was our "normal" for the moment.

One pattern that lasted for four years was his morning trek down the driveway to retrieve the newspaper. Even in the coldest winter days, first thing each morning, he put on his jacket and boots and stepped outside. Sometimes he would walk up to the folded paper and stand there looking at it because his brain was slow in telling his body to bend down and pick it up.

If he didn't get back in the house within five minutes, I'd prepare myself to go out and help him. When he saw me checking on him, he'd look at me, look down at the paper, and then look away. That meant, "I've got this."

He often had the paper in his hand before I could get my jacket on to assist him.

Another item that never needed to get on the list was the laundry. Larry loved to wash clothes, and he did it without any prompting, even if a load was only a few items. When our old dryer literally burned up, smoke and all, Larry and I went to buy a new washer and dryer. The salesperson asked how often we washed our clothes. I told him a load or two each day, and he quickly moved us from the sale machines to the more expensive commercial ones.

"These will last you a lifetime," he said.

How long is that, exactly? I thought to myself.

It took some Post-it notes to mark the settings on the new machines to get Larry back in the laundry business. Folding the laundry was not part of his service.

It was so tempting to "test" him. Did he remember? Could he still do it? Did he know or not? And some days he was able to do one thing and unable the next day. Without awareness at the time, I wasn't testing him; I was testing to prove to myself that he wasn't getting worse. The problem was that my lack of patience didn't allow him to process at a slower speed. Admittedly, there were days when my frustration overtook me. It took time and practice to adjust to our new way of being.

He could not stop himself from putting my expensive fry pan in the dishwasher when he loaded it after every meal. Whenever I saw this happen, I would go into a rant in my head. *Why can't he remember this simple thing?* As time went on, I just expected to see that fry pan in the dishwasher. I would take a breath and quietly pull it out. Of course, there was the silent, *Oy.* Yes, another small thing, but it was so easy to forget he wasn't doing this intentionally. He was doing the best he could.

There were some things that we'd had no choice but to change in our lifestyle. Travel became more challenging, which meant no fun. We had to cut way back. We stopped buying concert tickets with our friends because the music would relax me, and I'd fall asleep in my seat from exhaustion. We had to give up so many things that were once so easy to pick up and do. Even going to the mall required considerations around timing, carrying a big enough bag for his Depends, parking in a good location, and keeping a watchful eye at all times. It was how it had to be.

But I kept trying anything that would keep Larry independent—anything he could do without stressing me. Some worked better than others.

To say Larry was attached to his iPhone and Apple Watch would be an understatement. Most of the time, they were toys rather than tools. In my attempt to keep Larry feeling in control of his life, I set alarms on his iPhone and Apple Watch to remind him of bathroom breaks and appointments. While I wanted him to respond to these alarms, I doubted he would. So, ridiculously, I linked his alarms to my Apple Watch which meant every two hours, my phone or watch would notify me of bathroom time or whatever. Alarms were going off constantly, driving me nuts, while Larry never paid any attention to them. I never could figure out how to make this system work. It was probably something we should have started much earlier. It was too late to be an effective solution.

One day I took Larry with me to my acupuncture appointment. It was only a thirty-minute treatment. He sat down in the waiting area and began to use his phone to read the news. It all seemed normal when I went into my treatment room. While I was on the table with needles from head to toe, my phone kept ringing and ringing from my purse in the corner. One call would stop, and another would start. I had to do something, so needles and all, I carefully got up and answered the phone. It was Sarah checking if everything was OK. Apparently, while playing with his phone, Larry set off the SOS, which then called both of my daughters as if it was an emergency. They panicked and began calling me. My treatment was ruined—a deep breath, a laugh, and a reminder that he didn't mean to do it.

Not only was it important to maintain daily routines that seemed normal, but for our family, keeping long-held traditions kept all of us feeling that our life was not broken—it was predictable.

Our traditions were familiar to Larry. We kept them up, modifying as needed over the years to accommodate his changes and to keep him in the middle of the action.

Every August, our entire family took a trip to Lake Superior, even the summer before Larry passed away. Every Sunday, we'd FaceTime his brother in Florida at ten in the morning. Every Valentine's Day, I'd receive a beautiful card from Larry with a handwritten romantic love note. The last two Valentine's Days of his life, I pulled out old cards he gave to me and read his sweet notes while he sat at my side listening to words he had written. You can imagine the tears that flowed.

By far, the most lasting and impactful tradition was our Friday Shabbat dinners with the entire family. Because we're Jewish, Friday evening is special and a breather by design. It begins with the lighting of candles, a glass of wine, challah bread, and a full dinner. My matzo ball soup is a staple. Both Larry and I grew up with this tradition, and it has continued to this day, even without him.

Larry's job was to set the table for our Shabbat gathering. Around four o'clock, he'd begin to fidget, ready to get started. Everyone would assemble around five thirty, and he would be ready for them. The biggest challenge for him was remembering how many places to set at the table, something that rarely changed from the nine of us. He did pretty well for several years. If something wasn't right, we'd ignore it. As his abilities decreased, his need for direction and assistance increased. He started setting the table in very interesting ways. By the end, my daughter would set the table under Larry's watchful eye.

Seated at his place at the head of the table, he would look over his family gathered around him. Without question, this was the thing he loved the most.

Before we light the Sabbath candles, our family's tradition is to cover our eyes and take a deep breath to let go of the past week. I always had a lot to let go of, so it took me a while. Then we would all chant the blessings to welcome a new week. I could see Larry mouthing the words he had spoken for seventy-plus years. They were words he never forgot. Over dinner we had fun conversations around the table, always trying to include Larry. A little wine would loosen all of us after a hard week. In fact, Larry was so relaxed from wine at times that he knocked over his wine glass. That was remedied with stemless wine glasses—a little tweak.

One Shabbat, Nate suggested something he had learned at school that became part of our weekly tradition. He asked us to share one good thing about the past week and one thing we had learned. Everyone took it seriously, which really surprised me. When we got around the table to Larry, it would have been easy to skip him, but instead, we turned to him.

Nate would say, "Papa, it's your turn."

I'd prompt him and repeat, "Larry, what was one good thing for you this week?"

We all could have predicted his answer.

He looked at me and said, "You."

Then I'd ask him the second question, "What did you learn this week?"

He gave another predictable answer. "I love my family."

This went on for weeks, until words got too hard for him, but we knew what he would have said. The scrapbook moment of this little exercise has become part of our family's collective memories. Even now as we go around the table, I'm pretty certain that someone is having a flashback and hearing Larry's voice in their mind while feeling the warmth of his love.

Friday nights hold many lasting memories for our family, made even more significant because Larry took his last breath at five thirty on a Friday eve. As always, we were all gathered around him.

With all the dementia complications that kept surprising us, it was comforting to know that there were some things that were predictable and familiar. Even if I knew that the patterns were temporary, we had periods when living felt somewhat normal. It was a continual trial and error process to find things that would keep Larry going and doing. And every day, I watched him push himself as hard as I pushed him. Together with my family, life went on, changed perhaps, but still worth living.

Doing, Helping, Living

Note to self: It would be so easy to slip into "existing" rather than "living."

Every doctor Larry met along the dementia trail knew he was an attorney because he made sure to tell them. He always added that his fee was $325 an hour. Jokingly, he gave that rate for anything you would ask him to do, even if it was to take out the garbage.

"Dad, can you do me a favor?"

"Yes. It will be $325 an hour."

It never changed from the day he retired. When he couldn't speak, I took over these comments, to his delight. It was important that people knew he was an attorney and didn't view him as "less than."

This presented a puzzle for me as I tried to figure out how to keep him doing something that would make him feel good about himself and get him out of the house so I had some space. Our life could not be all about tasks, sitting in front of the TV, or running errands. Sure, he was retired and had dementia, but for forty-six years, Larry did what he loved—help people. I believed he could still help people.

Since I was basically Larry's activities director, each day I needed a good answer to his question, "What are we going to do today?" The challenge was getting the "we" out of the question and figuring out what he was going to do to keep both of us happy.

The underlying motivation for my push to find activities for Larry was my fear that if he wasn't doing something, he would act ill and lose interest in life. The focus had to be on what he could still do that would make him feel like he mattered, while at the same time recognizing that he could never become something he never was. He wasn't a chatty guy, and he would have hated a club or day program. He wasn't a creative, so arts or craft projects wouldn't work.

One of the first activities we tried for Larry months after his diagnosis and retirement was auditing an accounting class at the community college nearby. Every Tuesday from nine to noon he had a place to be. I have no idea how well he did, but he was using his brain, which kept him from thinking about losing it, and he had an answer when family asked, "Whatcha do today?" That lasted one semester.

We needed something else. I knew the head of a program called Wills for Heroes. This organization places lawyers out into the community to prepare simple wills for first responders, including police and firefighters. Again, this was in the first year of our life with dementia, so he was still able to do a lot. Even knowing Larry's condition, my friend was more than willing to have him help. He couldn't draft the wills, but they needed notaries and witnesses, so that's what he did for almost a year.

At first, he drove himself to the sites, always dressed professionally with his notary seal in its leather case, secure in his shirt pocket. After a day when he got lost, I drove him to the sites, even if it meant dropping him off and then killing four hours till I could pick him up. As long as they would have him, I got him there.

When he'd come home, I'd always ask, "How many wills did you witness this time?"

It didn't matter what answer he gave. It made him feel like he helped others. I reminded him about the great service he was providing for families.

We kept Wills for Heroes going till I got a call from the organizer.

"We really like Larry, but it's getting too difficult for him to remember the process. He can do it, he just needs someone to get him started, which we don't have time for."

I don't know who was more disappointed, Larry or me.

Nevertheless, it was a great first step into volunteering.

I learned from experience that volunteering is tricky for people with dementia. But the opportunities are out there. It's worth the effort to try to find organizations where volunteers require little, if any, supervision.

We had a couple of mismatches like shelving books in the library or stocking shelves at a food bank; those didn't work because Larry needed constant direction. I knew this because I stayed in touch with the organizers to make sure he could be helpful. The last thing I wanted was for Larry to be a disruption to the important work these organizations do.

Luckily, I found a spot for him that lasted two years at Second Harvest Heartland, an extensive food distribution center near our home.

Volunteering for them filled hours of Larry's time, and the best part was that they liked having him come. I signed him up for a shift once a week and sometimes more. He would sort and pack potatoes, hot seal bags of dry beans, whatever they thought he could do. Sometimes when I'd pick him up, he smelled like a potato. It was a far cry from being an attorney, but I kept reminding him how many people he was feeding. Sure, there were blips. Occasionally he forgot his jacket or his hat—all minor in the scheme of things. When he got to a point where he couldn't drive there himself, I got him there however I could. Sometimes I'd go with him and pack the potatoes too. I wanted to see if he could still be helpful. That's how I found out he actually had a friend who looked forward to him coming. He called Larry "the quiet guy." It was a wonderful gig while it lasted.

He was active, and, just as when he was an attorney, he helped people in ways that made him feel important, even if it was packing potatoes.

Doing and helping in meaningful ways at home was a bit harder. We were on familiar territory, yet Larry wasn't capable of doing things like he had done in the past. It really did require supervision. Yet I tried.

For example, doing our taxes was always left up to Larry. It was one of his many responsibilities to which I paid no attention until I had to. In fact, observing him struggle for days and days with receipts and slips of paper all over his home office is what got me to have him tested for dementia. Until then, I wasn't aware of how he had lost his ability to process information.

Recognizing that he couldn't do it anymore meant I had to take over getting our tax information in order and hire a real accountant. I also knew that he would see me doing it and want to get into the game. It was "his job." So, for three tax seasons, I continued to engage him in the process—well, sort of. Needless to say, each year got a bit more complicated for both of us as he "assisted" me.

Whenever I thought of Larry working on taxes, I envisioned him sitting with his little adding machine. He loved using that tiny treasure, entering numbers and then hearing the noise of it grinding out totals on long strips of paper.

So in order to help me work on our taxes, I dug it out from his old office supplies, along with a roll of adding machine tape from his lifetime supply. I should mention that he had two identical adding machines, just in case one malfunctioned. Larry may have been the only person who used an adding machine after calculators and Excel spreadsheets took over.

We sat side by side at a big table, and I brought out all of the documents, including the hundreds of sales receipts that Larry insisted I collect every year to calculate sales tax. After I reviewed the papers for pertinent information and did my calculations, I handed him small stacks and asked him to add them up on his machine. He would enter the amounts and then hand me the strips with his totals, feeling important. He was doing something he had done hundreds of times before. He believed he was really contributing and that was important.

I really questioned the integrity of having him do this busywork. I guess you had to be there to see him clicking away on that little adding machine to know how happy he was. He was back into his world of work, a place where he felt good about himself.

It would have been so much easier to have Larry sit in his chair all day. And some days, I needed that to happen just to get my energy back. But I was committed to keeping him active. As long as my expectations of Larry's capabilities and capacity were realistic, we kept trying to find things he could do. Some would say my expectations were too high, but after assessing the risks versus the rewards, I'd ask myself, "What's the worst thing that could happen?" The best thing that could happen was easy to decipher. Larry would feel like he was still doing, helping, and living.

Identity Protection

Note to self: My family has teased me for years that they will inscribe on my tombstone, "She tried."

*L*arry wasn't a "car guy" like my son-in-law, but he was a guy who loved to drive his car. Driving represented his independence. At the beginning of his illness, he was still a good driver and I was certain he could run an errand and get back. After about a year, I knew he was still capable of driving well, but I worried he'd get lost if he was out and be unable to find his way home.

Something had to change, but unlike when the nurses advised deceit to accomplish a goal, it needed to follow the principles that were guiding me.

The change began in stages. We eased into it. I would say to him, "Why don't we take my car?" That meant I would drive. Since we went to most places together, this just became a pattern. His car sat in the garage. The keys were in a drawer as always. On one or two occasions, I had him back his car out to the end of the driveway and then into the garage again.

"It needs to be driven a bit," I'd say.

Knowing that Larry was never going to drive again, both for his safety and for others, I was concerned about how he would feel losing this important piece of his independence. It took a while for me to realize that for Larry it was also about his identity.

It's hard for me to believe that anyone treasured their driver's license as much as Larry, especially after his diagnosis. It had his name, his photo, and his birthdate. It represented the identity he was clinging to.

Then Larry's driver's license needed to be renewed on his birthday. I had an internal dilemma. *Did I renew it or just get a simple ID?*

He wasn't driving anymore, I told myself, *but if he gives up his license, it would mean his ability to drive had been taken away. Would he see it as a loss of his personhood?*

Could he stop driving without taking away his license?

The question really wasn't whether Larry can drive or not. The question was how would he feel if he was stripped of one of the most important items in his wallet—a representation of who he is.

That was the convincing point. Keeping his identity and his desire to stay in the action both came into play. I knew what had to be done.

We made an appointment to renew his license. To my amazement, he passed everything. I stood by his side and assisted where needed, and he walked out of there a fully licensed driver. But he never took the wheel again. When his shiny new driver's license came in the mail, it went right in front of his wallet. It was a terrible photo of him, but it was him, a symbol of something he still had—his identity.

The car keys were in the desk drawer as always, but Larry never took them out.

It was his car that was the bigger issue, but only because I made it so. Larry was very content to have the car just sitting in the garage. It meant things were the same. Being an impatient woman, I thought I should finalize things and get rid of it. But I was unsure. First, I called the insurance company to see what would be needed if it remained in the garage and was never driven. They had an easy solution—stop paying the premiums. It sat for two years, as I would say, "taking up space."

Then out of the blue a woman in one of my groups made a casual comment that she wanted to buy her husband a car as a gift. She was looking for an older Nissan Altima. My ears perked up because that was Larry's car.

"I might have one for sale."

"How much would you want for it?"

I had done a bit of research as to the worth of the car.

"Five thousand dollars."

"I could be interested!"

This would be a big decision and one I thought Larry needed to be part of, yet I was still uncertain of what we should do.

As I was writing this story, I called Sarah to get her recollections of our conversation about her dad's car.

"Mom, all I remember is that one minute you were selling it, the next minute you were keeping it for Max, then you were selling it. You had yourself in a circle."

She was right. I lost my compass.

The woman called.

"I'd like to come over to see the car." After a quick look she said, "I'll write you a check."

That was a little too fast for me. I hesitated. "Could you wait a day while I discuss it with Larry?"

I need to back up here to set the stage for what comes next. We were months away from taking our entire family on a very big vacation to San Diego. It would be expensive, and the five thousand dollars was talking to me. If Larry sold his car, that would be money he could contribute to the trip, something I knew he would feel good about.

So that's the context in which I presented the question to him. I wasn't trying to manipulate or convince him. I felt he needed to be part of the decision since it was his car.

"Larry, there is a woman who would like to buy your car for five thousand dollars."

He made no comment but had a skeptical look on his face.

"It would be nice to have the cash for our trip. What do you think?"

He was tracking the conversation.

"Do you think we should sell it to her?"

"Yes."

While not a convincing answer, I wasn't going to have him believe I sold his car without his knowledge, whatever his knowledge was.

The next afternoon the buyer came to take the car.

Still concerned about Larry feeling good about his car being sold, I had her make the check to him. She knew Larry before he got sick and was aware of his current condition. With kindness and understanding, she let him know that she would take good care of his car and that her husband would drive his important customers around in it. Then she presented him with the check. He looked at it and wasn't impressed. Then he watched his car leave the driveway forever.

Was it the right decision? I will never know. Did I believe I made the right decision? Not really, but I didn't know how to do it right so I could stay true to my compass.

It was done, but I wasn't done.

"Larry, let's put the check in your bank account. You need to endorse it first."

He signed the back of the check, and we deposited it at his bank.

Then there was one more step.

"Larry, we said the money would pay for part of the trip. Why don't you write a check to American Express to cover what we have already paid?"

He pulled out his treasured blue plastic checkbook, which he kept in his shirt pocket on most days. Then he scribbled a check to American Express and handed it to me. At this point, I'm not sure if I was still trying to make Larry feel good about the decision or if I was trying to make myself believe it was right.

The reality is, I never felt good about that decision, and I paid the price.

Once the car was no longer in the garage, Larry would constantly ask me, "Where is my car?" I should have known this was coming because whenever one of my family members took his car for one reason or another, Larry would start to look for it, even opening the garage door several times to see if it was back.

One day I had heard, "Where is my car?" one too many times. I was tired of telling him over and over that his car was sold. I thought he didn't understand that his car was sold or that he was still feeling upset about the loss, which, of course, made me feel awful. Even though I was ready to scream, I needed to end this question in a respectful way.

We pulled into the garage that day, and I saw a big piece of cardboard. I ran into the house, grabbed a fat marker, and in large letters wrote, "Car Sold." Then I put it on the front wall of the garage, easily seen when we drove in. For a few weeks after that, whenever we drove into the garage I would point to the sign and read it before he'd ask his question, and yes, probably with a bit of a tone. The sign stayed up for months as I gradually moved my car toward the center of the garage. And then the question faded as an issue.

It was only after telling my therapist about my "smart" solution that I realized I wasn't so smart after all.

"That wasn't the real problem," she said, with a knowing look in her eye.

"He stopped asking about his car," I argued.

"You have a two-car garage, and he expected to see two cars in there. That was his memory. It was a pattern established over years. That was how his brain worked."

"But I included him in the conversation about the sale."

"Yes, but that conversation unfolded over days. His car was gone for a while, and he probably thought it would return just like when the kids borrowed it. That was the pattern he knew."

I totally missed it. I misunderstood his dementia. He wasn't forgetting that I sold the car, he was trying to work out why the other car was missing.

I really tried on this one. My intentions were good, but I was asking myself the wrong questions. I was focused on keeping him in the action and preserving his feeling of independence and autonomy. What I didn't ask was, "What does Larry want or need?" I assumed he was suffering from no longer driving or from missing his car, but it didn't appear traumatic for him—as long as he was riding by my side and he still had his driver's license in his wallet.

Today, his license is sitting in a drawer where I can see it when I go to get something. Sometimes I take it out and hold it, looking at his silly photo, and think about what this loss was like for both of us. Sometimes I think back on memories of when he drove everywhere and I was the passenger. After I bought our new car, I joked that I never had a chance to ride in the passenger seat. Today, I'm still doing the driving, and the passenger seat is empty.

Almost Normal

Note to self: I got myself refocused this afternoon and had a lovely time with Larry as we sat on the deck. The bird feeders are finally set, and the cardinals and goldfinches are back, which makes us happy to just sit together and watch them.

Not everything in those five years after Larry's diagnosis was doom and gloom. It didn't take much to lighten the mood as long as I accepted that "fun" was going to look and feel different.

When we were driving around town, Larry and I played a little game. Even though he wasn't behind the wheel, he was still paying attention, almost like he was driving in his mind. A cute scrapbook moment of mine is the way he would evaluate how I stopped at stop signs.

If I didn't meet his standards of a complete stop, he would say, "That wasn't a stop."

When he no longer could talk, he would give me one of his disapproving looks.

Sometimes I'd encourage him with, "How was that stop?"

Or I'd preempt him and say, "I know. That wasn't a great one."

Since we had a stop sign right in front of our driveway, I had many opportunities to play the stop sign game with him. After a while, I realized that while he seemed to gloat with his reaction, he may not have seen this as a game but a way to show he still knew how to drive. Either way, it made him happy and made me smile.

Larry was at times distant, but there were other times when he was present—as long as I made it easy for him. My goal was always to keep him from feeling broken and me feeling like he was still Larry. We both needed that.

Because Larry looked good until the last year, most people couldn't tell he was different. I think he still saw his old self too, at least when he looked in the mirror. Any time he could, he'd remind his bald brothers that he had more hair than them and that his was still black.

You would never say that Larry was a fashionista, but he never dressed sloppily. Any day, at any time, he chose to wear what we called his "dressed like a lawyer" uniform. His closet was full of starched, button-down "lawyer shirts" and khaki pants. This was what he wore every workday after business casual dress came in fashion around 1990. He was thrilled to give up his tie and suit for the office, only bringing them out for days in court.

Even on days when we would just sit around the house, he wore either his uniform or a nice shirt and jeans. I could never get him to be comfortable in athletic clothing, and he wouldn't be seen in sweatpants. As much as my life would have been simplified in those last years if he gave up on jeans with a belt to wear elastic-waist pants, I was secretly happy that he still wanted to retain his "look." And I really liked seeing him that way. He looked like Larry, which of course I desperately wanted him to be.

Dementia didn't stop him from keeping his old-fashioned manners either. He always opened doors for me, at least until his concept of space diminished and he would open a door even if there was a little kid in danger of getting knocked over. I needed watchful eyes. When we went for walks, he insisted on walking on the street side to protect me. That was what gentlemen did, and he kept on doing it. All OK with me. We were walking together.

One thing that Larry counted on was having his wallet in his back pocket. He wasn't fully dressed without it. When he didn't have much to carry around in a big wallet anymore, I bought a thin one. In it was one credit card with a bank limit, a five-dollar bill, plus five one-dollar bills. Two or three times during the day, he would take his wallet out of his pocket, open it, and check to see that everything was in it. Then he would place it back in his pocket, feeling satisfied.

For as long as he could, Larry didn't want to stop showing us that he was still the "guy." Before he was diagnosed, whenever we went to a restaurant, Larry would grab the check to pay as soon as it arrived. And of course, when we were with the family, everyone expected him to pay. After his diagnosis, he continued to reach for the check and then proudly pull his credit card from his wallet. Having retained his math abilities for a long time, he could still figure the tip and add the total, then sign it with his classic signature. I'd covertly review the check before it left the table. This lasted for a couple of years. Ultimately it had to stop, but while he could do it, he paid. It made him feel important and still in control of some aspect of his life. It was a sign that some things were as they once were, and that seemed to delight him. It delighted me as well because it felt familiar.

Sometimes situations required a bit of creative thinking to make things seem right.

When a TSA agent asked us to show our driver's licenses at the airport checkpoint, Larry turned to me with his frightful blank stare. I could feel my panic button go off. He had just used it to get his boarding pass but couldn't recall where he put it after that. We were asked to step out of the line till we found it. Larry just stood there, frozen.

"Check your wallet," I commanded.

He did.

"Check again."

He did.

"Check your pockets."

He checked his pockets and wallet over and over as my heart raced and we got closer and closer to our flight departure.

I remember thinking if I started feeling deep in his pockets, I'd be arrested.

Then quietly Larry reached into his shirt pocket and pulled out his driver's license.

"OY!"

After this extremely stressful episode at the airport, I made an important adjustment. I never wanted either of us to repeat the panic of our experience at the TSA checkpoint.

I vowed that would not happen again, so I photocopied his treasured driver's license and laminated it for his wallet. Then I kept the real one in my purse. Larry seemed just fine with that and so was I. One potential hassle was eliminated as we continued to travel together.

We had many ordinary days when we were doing errands which frequently included a stop at Barnes & Noble. As soon as we'd walk in, Larry would head straight to the newest thriller written by one of his favorite authors and then hand me a book to purchase. It made perfect sense because that's what we always did in the past. I also knew that the book was never going to be read. Yet I couldn't stand the thought of not buying him a book and having him look at me with "I don't understand" written on his face. So, we purchased another book, usually a cheaper paperback, to be stacked by his bedside. It was an easy way for him to feel that life was as it should be. Yes, he kept "reading," but only the same book. He was content just looking at the pages.

It was hard to tell what made Larry happy, but I was willing to try anything that I thought he would enjoy. He built almost every Lego architecture kit I could find. Then that got too hard. He liked to play solitaire on his iPad, until he couldn't manage the technology. He seemed to enjoy bowling on the Wii with the boys, but after beating them at two games, he was done. I kept trying.

In those first two years, there were little moments where Larry's sweet side would show up.

When I was sick and needed gallbladder surgery, Larry was upset. He could sense that something was wrong. To my surprise, as I was lying in the pre-op bed, he seemed fully cognizant of what was happening. In fact, while the doctor was talking to me, Larry kept rubbing my feet. When I was wheeled into surgery, I looked at him and said, "Goodbye." His quick response was, "Don't say goodbye, say I'll see you later." While a real scrapbook moment, it once again highlighted the unpredictability of dementia and was a good reminder that sweet moments could be found, especially when I had a loving man by my side.

After a life together of constant activity, big trips, and fun parties, it seems unbelievable that these seemingly little things would be noted as "almost normal." I'm grateful that both of us were able to find some light in the darkness as we walked through our dementia life.

Here is a note I found in my journal that captures the feeling of those early years.

Larry was home alone much of the day. When I came home tonight, I found an almost old Larry. He was in a good mood, having checked off all the items on his list. We had a glass of wine over dinner and began to talk about how he was doing. Of course, he still thinks he is just fine. He said, "You don't see anything wrong with me, do you?" I

decided to answer honestly. I told him what I ob-
served, the changes I had seen, the missing parts of
him, the sadness and depression he was showing.
He claimed he was not depressed but agreed he was
"lost" and couldn't find a purpose. He said he was
"stupid." This made me sad. I used that to say, "You
are not stupid. You still have all the knowledge in
your brain. It just gets messed up sometimes." It was
a moving and honest conversation. The wine helped
a lot. Then, I gave him the gift I bought for him—a
2,000+ piece Lego set. I told him that, while it was
expensive, I've been spending so much on myself, I
felt it was time to get him something, too. I could
tell immediately that he loved it. He wanted to
begin working on it right after dinner.

In the early days after learning of Larry's diagnosis, I would look at couples walking hand in hand as they strolled by the lake or in the mall, deep in conversation. It looked so "normal," and I would get very jealous.

Somewhere, I heard spoken, "Normal is the thing many don't notice until it changes." Our normal was constantly changing, and I noticed it daily. I realized I had taken for granted how good normal once felt. I also realized how little attention I had paid to those small things that made life seem right. As difficult as it was, I had to accept that my life would never be as it once was, but it could feel almost normal and right for the moment.

The Scarlet "D"

Dementia-ism

Note to therapist: I've become a skeptic of doctors, yet I need them. I feel like even an infected toenail could be attributed to "the progression of dementia."

Her response: It can be true if the pace of change in a chronic illness happens often enough it becomes conventional "wisdom." But since I've known you I've become convinced that the Marofskys are immune to convention.

*L*arry was a very sick man. From the first diagnosis, and for the next five years, I would observe a change in his health then ask questions. That usually led to us seeing a specialist who would add one more diagnosis to his already long list.

Two variants of frontotemporal dementia (FTD) robbed him of his ability to communicate and ultimately his ability to move his body. Primary progressive aphasia ultimately silenced him. His final diagnosis was another kind of FTD—motor neuron disease or ALS—that weakened his muscles, limited his movement, and eventually caused respiratory failure.

All are miserable diseases individually, but together, a crappy situation. We saw many doctors over five years.

These appointments became a great source of stress, discouragement, and wasted time for our family because many of the doctors we saw had a condition themselves. It's called "dementia-ism." This is a real descriptor I found in a UK medical journal defined as "the denial of equitable care for those living with dementia." My personal definition is: Since Larry has a dementia diagnosis, anything that goes wrong is because of his dementia—even if it isn't.

Because I refused to believe that all of Larry's medical conditions were related to dementia, I was on a constant quest for answers and continually running up against doctors with dementia-ism. From these encounters, I feel confident saying it isn't the science of medicine that is the issue, but the doctors who often have their biases and interpretations of the science. They use checklists for diagnosis, have their own agendas, and many are not good listeners. We even met some doctors who were downright arrogant and disrespectful. If the patient has dementia on their health record, that is what doctors see first, and sometimes it is all they see.

Here is a prime example of how a doctor at the university dismissed us from the beginning.

Larry's family has an unusual genetic disease that has the potential of causing dementia-like symptoms and for which there could be a treatment. Still trying to uncover any rock that might provide something resembling a "cure," we were referred to a specialist who was doing extensive research on this disease. His primary work was with children, but one day a week he saw adults.

When Larry, Eve, and I checked in for our appointment, we were escorted to his office and told to sit in three chairs that were designed for kindergarteners. We were basically seated on the floor. The doctor and his assistant sat in adult-sized chairs and looked down at us as they spoke, but they weren't really talking to us. They were having a medical consultation with each other while we were in our little chairs, observing their interaction as we strained our necks to look up.

In the end, the doctor informed us that there was a costly treatment we could consider. Then he added, "Since Larry has dementia, it is unlikely we would see much improvement."

Hearing this, I thought to myself, *And why would we even consider doing this?*

He didn't wait for a response; I could tell he was getting excited, almost like a dog seeing a bone. "We could do a brain scan as a baseline, then give him the treatment to see if it's working."

"There are similar studies going on in the UK . . ." Then without completing his thought he turned to his computer and began showing us images of brain scans—other people's brains.

He was very eager for Larry to become another specimen for his research.

It was all ridiculous and disrespectful, and I was angry. Dementia-ism!

One colossal example of dementia-ism is a story about how we finally found out that Larry had Guillain-Barré syndrome (GBS), a rapid onset of muscle weakness, causing paralysis. It's a story about my fight against dementia-ism, which meant encountering many doctors who blew it. GBS is reversible with early treatment, but if it's not treated, it can be life-threatening—we came close.

Larry and I took a trip to Sedona with Eve and Lawrence for Larry's seventy-third birthday, three years after his diagnosis. He started off great and hiked and walked all over. Then he said his legs hurt, and he began to have difficulty walking, so we left for home early.

The day after we got home, he started limping, and we went to urgent care to check it out. They examined him, ran a few tests, but quickly said something like, "It's most likely the progression of dementia."

I accepted this but didn't like it. The next day, Larry was really having trouble walking. His legs weren't working, and he stumbled a lot. I called and got him an appointment that afternoon with our clinic and pushed the doctor to look deeper.

He checked for a blood clot with an ultrasound but found nothing. Again, we heard, "Probably signs that his dementia is progressing."

Feeling crazy, I helped Larry, who was having tremendous difficulty walking, get to the car.

On day three, Larry was worse. I rushed him to the emergency room, and his internist met us there. After a brief exam and lots of questions, his doctor was stumped. It seemed his only recourse was classic dementia-ism.

Apologetically, he said, "I'm afraid this is how it's going to be. I'll order home care."

All this time, I'm saying to myself, dementia doesn't work this fast. You don't walk one day, and three days later, your legs are paralyzed.

Later that same day, while on the phone, reluctantly arranging home care, I looked over and saw Larry on the floor. He had fallen trying to get up. That was it!

Sarah and I dragged him back to the ER. I was determined to have him admitted and get an answer. I wasn't going to go home with him. I'm no doctor, but I knew it wasn't dementia, and I needed someone to believe me.

That's when I called my therapist to tell her I couldn't make our appointment.

"I'm with Larry and Sarah in the emergency room again. It's packed in here and I don't know when we will be seen. It's the third time in three days and I still can't get any answers. Larry is getting worse!"

Hearing the panic in my voice and clearly concerned she said, "Myrna, if they can't give you answers to the same questions—what is causing him to fall and what can be done about it—I think you should leave that hospital now. Your questions are important ones."

Then she recommended a hospital across town where she knew colleagues and their emergency room procedures.

"They will get you in quickly."

Determined to find an answer, I followed her advice. Sarah and I schlepped poor Larry from one hospital to another. My therapist met us there.

From her professional training in hospitals and rehab facilities, she was convinced dementia wasn't the problem and thought it might be GBS, cautioning us that if so, it would be serious.

Thankfully, we were seen within minutes. A wonderful young resident doctor met us and within an hour, the spinal tap confirmed it was GBS. Treatment began immediately, and we saved Larry's life.

A few more days undiagnosed, and this disease that travels from the toes upward to the respiratory system could have been fatal.

It wasn't dementia!

Larry had a long road back. He met his physical therapy goals in the hospital then moved to an acute rehab facility before being discharged.

All during his stay in a rehab facility, he was viewed through the lens of dementia-ism.

One doctor pulled me out in the hallway and said, "His dementia is going to make this difficult. I hope you are thinking long term. It would be a good time to get his name on a memory care facility waiting list."

Even during outpatient physical therapy, I kept hearing doubts about whether Larry could follow the exercises and if he could remember them. They'd ask me, "Do you think he can?" Well, he could, and he did. After months of hard work and determination, he recovered his mobility completely.

Was it just easier for these doctors to put the blame on dementia? Why did I have to fight to get proper attention?

These miserable experiences convinced me to fight dementia-ism as much as possible.

As Larry's condition got more complicated, we were going from one specialist to another. That meant that I was the only one who knew the entire picture of Larry's health. The computer records told some facts, but I needed to fill in with observations and anecdotal details that might play into assessment and possible treatment. I didn't wait for them to ask or to simply make assumptions that dementia was the problem.

Like everything else, I took charge by preparing for these appointments in ways that steered away from dementia, always questioning to determine the causes of Larry's condition.

That led me to prepare in a different way. It's something I do for myself now when I see a doctor. Before every appointment, I wrote down what I observed and what I wanted out of the visit. My questions required both direct factual answers and open-ended ones, designed to help me better handle our situation.

Some of my questions may have seemed inconsequential to a medical professional, but the answers were important for me to know.

Since they never talked directly to Larry, I took the reins.

"Here is why we are here, and this is what I want to understand."

"I'd like to go over Larry's medications to see if any can be eliminated or if there could be contraindications because . . ."

"Larry's breath is bad. This is new. I'd like to check to see if there is a medical reason."

Note that I was clear on the outcomes I came for. I wanted more than one- or two-word answers, and, for sure, I didn't want to hear it was his dementia progressing—unless it really was.

What I asked for was a dialogue, which usually threw them off their natural course, not to mention their schedule. I remember one doctor who actually liked the challenge and offered to do some research and get back to me. The benefit of my approach was that I became an integral part of Larry's health care.

I'm pleased to say that I found the right team in the end—thanks to referrals from my business network. It didn't change the outcome, but when Larry was in big trouble, we were in good hands.

Larry's primary doctor told me, "Larry is so lucky to have you as an advocate."

What I think he really meant was that I was a pushy woman who made him work. Yet I wonder if I put Larry through more than necessary. I tried to do the best for him, but without medical guidance I could trust, I was chasing unknowns.

My therapist and I didn't know the term dementia-ism when I was dealing with it but we knew what it was. We identified it time and time again. Many of our conversations involved sorting out what to challenge, what to accept, and often what to do next. I can't imagine how lonely it would have been not to have someone to talk to about this. When I was feeling crazy, my therapist was there to listen and validate not only my feelings but also my observations.

Dementia-ism from doctors caused a great deal of unnecessary angst for me, and, if not addressed, it could have had disastrous consequences for Larry. My antennas were tuned into anyone who saw the scarlet "D" on Larry's forehead before taking the time to learn more.

Questioning the wisdom of doctors wasn't how I grew up. Doctors were worshipped, especially if they were Jewish. Their word was never questioned. But from many experiences over many years I understand that medicine is as much an art as a science. It is the doctors who have the ability to paint whatever picture they are tuned into. Maybe I was too skeptical, but not when it came to my husband's life.

Silent but Not Gone

Note to self: I always try to bring Larry into conversations, saying, "Isn't that right, Larry?" Occasionally others catch on and start addressing him or even mentioning his name once or twice.

If he could, Larry would say to them, "I'm still here."

L arry hated when people acted like he was invisible. Without realizing it, our friends had mild cases of dementia-ism. Even when sitting right next to him, people would talk around him without providing any eye contact. I couldn't let that continue.

It felt risky to say, "Please speak to him," but I did. I had to think about the emotional withdrawal that Larry must have felt being left out of conversations, especially if they were about him.

This got worse as complications from his speech impediments of dysphagia and apraxia took more and more from him. Actually, his cognition and ability to understand was more accessible than his ability to form words. He understood directions, often knew what was being said to him, and was able to follow short conversations. He just couldn't respond or make facial expressions.

Of all the physical losses Larry endured, his silence and his inability to make a genuine smile were probably the most emotionally upsetting to both of us. We spent over fifty years talking about life, making decisions, laughing at our kids, and—in Larry's case—making funny faces at our baby grandsons. Then over the last two years of his life, all of this progressively disappeared.

First he would stutter, "Whata, whata . . ." but he would get a sentence out. Then the stuttering became garbled words. Our grandsons called it "Papa talk" because we all had to interpret what he was trying to say. Even as speaking was becoming very hard for him, he still let me know he was my sweetheart.

"How do I look?" I'd ask, hoping to get him to notice me.

Then realizing he was ignoring me, he would look up and say, "You . . . you . . . look beautiful."

Ultimately, speaking became so difficult that he stopped trying, and in his final two years he was basically silent.

As upsetting as aphasia was for Larry, it was excruciating for me. I'm an extrovert who enjoys a lively conversation. Admittedly, I usually did most of the talking in our family because Larry had always been a man of few words. But when he spoke, we listened.

He may have been silent, but he still had his opinions and desires, and his deep brown eyes told us so. After all the years we were together, I knew him well and could recognize his satisfaction and his discontent easily just by looking at his face. When I said something he disagreed with, he had no difficulty letting me know. All it took was one of his looks and a slight tilt of his head.

I love the story about the time we went to the bank to put my name on his account. I did all the talking because it had become too difficult for him. But it was Larry's account which meant he had to sign some things. I could see he enjoyed sitting there, pen in hand, ready to sign his name. He was an attorney after all, and this was a transaction. At the conclusion of our business, we stood to leave. I could read from Larry's eyes and posture that he wasn't done.

"You want to shake the banker's hand, don't you?"

The very astute young banker stood up immediately, reached for Larry's hand, and shook it gingerly.

"Thank you for your business, sir."

I think that was one of Larry's best days. He was treated as he had always been.

To our surprise, there were a few amazing times when he willed himself to say something that shocked us.

One of those times occurred at a momentous event for my grandson Max. From the minute Max was born, Larry started calculating how old we would be when Max had his bar mitzvah, a ceremony where a thirteen-year-old boy becomes a "Jewish man." For grandparents it is all about pride and pure joy.

Max didn't have a bar mitzvah. At least not a traditional one.

When he was around eleven years old, he began to suffer from depression, which was hard to believe and even harder to manage. Studying for his bar mitzvah had to stop. Happily, by the time Max was thirteen, he was well on the road to recovery, but there was no talk of him having a ceremony.

It was also a year when Larry had lost most of his ability to speak.

Being "the best Nana," I had a need to make age thirteen memorable for Max —in a Jewish way. That turned into a major project he began on his thirteenth birthday and completed one year later. We called it Max's Mitzvah Project. He was doing mitzvahs—in Yiddish meaning "good deeds"—then recording what he did and why it was important to him. Sarah helped me make a special book about this project, including tributes from others.

It was a wonderful project to do together. Larry's illness couldn't distract me from the important relationship that Max and I have.

That project in itself became something to remember, but a real and incredible scrapbook moment came later.

Wanting to connect what Max had accomplished to a real bar mitzvah, I contacted our rabbi and asked if we could have a gathering with Max and his family in her office so she could hear about what we did. As expected, the rabbi was wonderful and asked Max all about the project, letting him know there were many ways to have a bar mitzvah.

"Max, this project was your way of achieving the milestone," she said before asking Max about the details of his experience.

Max gave her mostly one-word answers, but he impressed us when he said the values he learned were now part of how he lives his life.

And then he turned and pointed at me and said, "Plus, she made me do it."

We all praised him, but, as a teen, he didn't know how to receive the compliments. Still, there was no doubt in anyone's mind that he was feeling good about himself.

As the meeting was ending, I noticed that Larry was trying to get into the action. I looked at him and asked if he wanted to say something. I worried because this was a time when he could hardly speak a clear word. He leaned forward. Then, with tremendous effort, he willed himself to speak with mumbled words which we all understood.

"Max, I'm proud of you."

No one could say a thing. We were all fighting back tears.

Larry loved Max with all his heart and soul, and he wasn't going to be left out of a chance to let him know that. It was also another reminder that parts of Larry's brain were still working and, most importantly, he was still with us. There were no photos that day, just full hearts. That is the staying power of memories made from scrapbook moments.

A year after Larry passed away, our twin grandsons had real bar mitzvahs. Well, sort of real, as it was on

Zoom in their living room during the pandemic. As they led the service, Larry's photo was right behind them on the bookcase, looking as if he was saying, "I'm here." He loved those boys and would have been sitting there as the proud Papa. Even though he wasn't physically with us, we knew he was there—silent but not gone.

I never thought about the beauty of silence until Larry was silenced. Unless the family was over, our house was very quiet, and to my amazement I learned to enjoy just being in Larry's presence. We didn't need words to communicate.

The Fourth Question

Note from my therapist: Chronic illness is isolating. And at no time is isolation felt more keenly than when in the company of others who do not know how to even try to understand your experience.

Recently I received an email from an acquaintance about a meeting we had attended together. At the bottom she added a postscript that said, *I just talked to a close friend of mine who is sixty-nine and has been diagnosed with early Parkinson's and mild cognitive decline. I'm going to try to stick with her through this. We are going to start walking in the mall as much as possible with this cold weather. How can I be there for her? Any ideas or tips? Her mom and grandmother had bad Alzheimer's disease.*

As one who doesn't shy away from telling others what to do or offering an opinion, I started my response with a bulleted list of suggestions. Then I stopped. I realized a list was the last thing she needed. I certainly knew that.

DELETE.

Here is what I wrote back: *Being her good friend is the best advice I can give. Talk about other things before you ask about her illness but understand that she is probably terrified. Being present and part of her life is a gift. Keep her whole as long as you can. Don't ask what she needs. If it feels right, do it, even if it's simply a hug. She is lucky you are in her life.*

I would never have written that response if I hadn't learned from my own experiences, especially from things that irritated me. My friends and associates were my age or younger. Most had healthy partners and were in good health themselves. There were few that understood my life and even fewer who, while they tried, knew how to be my good friend.

Over the course of Larry's illness, our life started to become filled with annoyances and frustrations, even from those who cared about us and others who tried to be helpful. A minor annoyance, yet a good example, is when I met friends for coffee or lunch or when I'd run into someone I knew at the grocery store.

"Great to see you; how is Larry doing?"

"So, tell me what's going on. How is Larry?"

"What's new with Larry?"

"Hi, how are things at home?"

They were ignoring the fact that there was more to me than Larry. They didn't realize that I was out and away from him for a reason. It was my precious time. I needed relief and something else to talk about.

And the one that really got to me was, "Are you taking care of yourself?"

My answer was a dismissive, "I'm doing the best I can."

I was taking care of myself, dammit! Or at least I was making an attempt.

It may seem ungrateful and crazy to even bring this up. My friends and acquaintances would never understand how these questions bothered me. But they did!

The harder realization was that I was also part of the problem. If someone asked, "How is Larry?" I could never honestly answer, "He is OK." He wasn't. I'd make things worse by going into a long narration of the current situation, which was usually awful. I couldn't stop myself because there was a lot on my mind, and I lived in a silent home. The term used today is TMI—too much information. As I spoke about how Larry's condition had become more and more difficult, my friends never knew how to respond. Most would reach for a hug. Sadly, an event that was supposed to be a needed social outing became a pity party.

After a frustrating evening with a group of friends, I brought this to a Wednesday therapy session. As we problem-solved together, my therapist and I came up with an idea we started calling the "Fourth Question." That meant I actually had to train others by redirecting our conversations from the beginning, trying for three topics before Larry even came up. Sometimes I would greet my friends or peers and ask if we could start by talking about something other than Larry.

"I'm so glad we could get together. I really needed a break from thinking about Larry. Let's just catch up on what you are doing first. Did you sign the lease on your building? Are you excited? What is your timeline?" or "How was Mexico? Was the weather good? I've never been there, what's it like?" Then I was ready for whatever came next.

Everyone was great about it—almost relieved. We always got to the Larry conversation, but I trained myself to do a Cliffs Notes version of the saga I was living.

I began to listen to the words I heard myself saying. Once I started removing language that painted a dreadful picture, I saw the energy lighten at a social hour. I also tried to set the tone of the conversation.

"I have hired a wonderful companion for Larry."

I hoped their response would be, "That's good to hear. What is she like?"

Now the conversation was diverted away from Larry. These adjustments made for a much more pleasant interaction.

Sometimes, especially with my friends, I'd make a quick opening by saying something about a headline in the news. That was always a great diversion because something was always happening to spew about.

Another well-meaning question that became one of my hot buttons was, "How can I help?" which goes along with, "I'm here for you" or, "Just let me know what you need."

When asked, I would freeze. I had nothing to ask for other than make Larry healthy again.

My reply was usually empty or, "There is nothing you can do."

A friend gave me Sheryl Sandberg's book called *Option B,* which she wrote after her husband suddenly passed away. I read it in one day because her story about resilience after a life-changing setback was so frank and honest. Sandberg talked about how people wanted to help her at a time when she didn't know what she needed. What stuck with me was how she appreciated the people who did what they felt in their hearts was right "just because." They didn't put the burden on her to ask for something. They didn't wait to be told. Some picked up the phone and called to say they were thinking of her or to check in to see how she was doing. Some people brought cookies without asking permission and set them on her doorstep. Others would drive across town just to give her a hug.

There was a lesson in that for me and something I could teach others. I was pretty good at taking care of my own needs. What felt right was knowing that someone cared, was thinking about us, and sending good wishes. I loved it when I'd get a text from Karen with a simple message: "Thinking of you," with a cute emoji. That little gesture was all it took for me to know I wasn't alone. My response to, "How can I help?" became, "Just knowing you are thinking of me is enough."

Some of those same kind and wonderful people called me on the first anniversary of Larry's death. They let me know I was on their mind. "This must be a hard day," they would say. A neighbor came over and brought me flowers and another sent me a beautiful card. I never did this for anyone, but I do it now. It is such a simple act of thoughtfulness.

Long ago, I realized that people can't read your mind. You need to ask for what you need. In my case, I not only had to ask, but I had to teach the people I interacted with and do it in a respectful way. To my delight, no one seemed offended; in fact, they thanked me for helping them help me.

Heart Warmers and
Heart Breakers

Note to therapist: I'm not sure what I expect from others, but the last thing I want is for them to feel sadness for us.

Her response: I don't know that you have to protect those who are there for you. I think you can trust them to be strong enough. And if anyone has a forlorn feeling or a sense of apprehension—that's OK—it is part of their humanity. Being human together is a good thing. Being present, even when someone is sad (maybe especially when someone is sad), is a gift, not a problem to be solved.

By now it's obvious that there was a lot going on in our lives and not much of it was fun. Sometimes I was so overwhelmed that I would look at Larry and breathlessly ask him, "What happened to our life?"

He would look up at me with his sad brown eyes. Along with the progression of an ugly illness came a tremendous amount of heartbreak for both of us as our lives were made difficult with many changes, hard decisions, and people everywhere.

It was the interactions with people that started me thinking about having an emotional bank account. People in my life, without even knowing it, were taking withdrawals and making deposits. In my mind I labeled them *Heart Warmers* and *Heart Breakers,* and crazy as it may sound, I kept a mental balance sheet, always trying to make the deposits exceed the withdrawals.

I use the word "heart" intentionally because that is where my emotional bank account was kept. Heart Breakers made my blood pressure rise, and Heart Warmers made my breathing easier.

There were Heart Breakers and Heart Warmers that left indelible marks on me over the years. I share them to highlight the differences and why it's important to embrace Heart Warmers and keep them close. For the Heart Breakers who never knew they had made a withdrawal, I chose to forget them and keep them at a distance. The hardest part was not to let Heart Breakers bankrupt my emotional bank account. It was something I had to continually work on.

Mike the Barber
Every two weeks for about thirty years, Mike would cut Larry's hair. Over the years they created a special bond so Larry followed him every time he moved to a new shop. His last move was a one-hour drive from our house.

When Larry was still driving, he would make the trip to Mike's shop every two weeks whether he needed a haircut or not. It was his version of having coffee with a friend. After he got lost trying to get there, I became the chauffeur. I knew that we needed to keep this routine no matter how inconvenient it was.

Before Larry's appointment, I'd have a quick phone conversation with Mike to let him know how Larry was doing. I didn't want him surprised.

Mike interacted with Larry as he always did. When we walked into the shop, Mike would hug Larry and guide him through the shampoo and cutting process, talking to him the entire time. I'd sit in the front and listen. Amazingly I would hear Larry respond in his limited way, even telling him we were heading to Florida in the coming week. And as he always did, Larry paid Mike with the twenty-five dollars I made sure was in his wallet. Even after Mike raised his fee for others, Larry's twenty-five dollars was graciously accepted.

Each time Larry got in the car after a haircut, I'd tell him how handsome he looked. Then he'd pull down the visor of the car to look in the mirror, turn to me, and beam.

Mike was more than a barber. He was a Heart Warmer. He helped Larry keep a part of his life that was familiar, and he did it with a generous soul right up to Larry's final haircut.

When the holidays came, Mike received a nice bonus with an appreciative card from me.

The Urologist

In my constant attempt to figure out what was going on with Larry's body, I took him to a urologist. His symptoms were atypical for Alzheimer's patients. As usual, Larry was dressed "business casual," even with his Depends underneath his expensive jeans. The doctor came in, and I had to give my usual disclaimer.

"My husband doesn't talk, but he understands everything. He gets upset if you don't talk to him."

The doctor then asked Larry questions, and Larry would look to me to answer. I explained the problem and gave the usual background. This forty-something-year-old doc was very impressed with Larry's fashionable jeans, and the fact that Larry was an attorney. He asked more questions about Larry's career than about his medical problem. Then he turned from his computer notes, looked at Larry, and just shook his head. I can't forget his insensitive remark that came next.

"This isn't right! You shouldn't have to be dealing with all of this. You should be enjoying life in Florida on the golf course. You earned it."

I thought to myself, *Gee thanks. Just what I wanted to hear! Don't you think I feel bad enough? Besides, Larry doesn't play golf.*

I should have ended the visit. I didn't.

After a brief examination, the doctor caught me off guard when he recommended surgery for Larry. When I asked that Larry be kept overnight in the hospital, "just in case," the doctor dismissed me, saying it was a "minor surgery" and that Larry should be "fine" at home.

I remember being frightened as I listened to him talk as if changing a catheter bag was no big thing.

I didn't fight that day. I'm not sure why, but it was probably because I would do anything to treat Larry's incontinence. Instead, I gave in.

Following the "minor" surgery, I took Larry home and ended up back in the emergency room within hours. It had become a "serious" situation.

Unknowingly, this doctor made big Heart Breaker withdrawals for me.

Strangers

There were many public bathroom nightmares as Larry became more confused and physically challenged. An understanding manager at our car dealership made a Heart Warmer deposit for me when Larry got locked in the men's single bathroom while our car was being serviced.

Larry was in there way too long, and I got worried. I knocked on the door several times, calling his name. It was clear that Larry was stuck and locked in. By this time, I was frantic and embarrassed. I found the manager of the dealership and explained what happened, emphasizing dementia, and asked if he could give me a key that would open the door.

Without any sign that this was an odd request, he said, "Well, let me look."

After checking every drawer and asking others, he couldn't find any key and looked genuinely concerned.

Having experience with a similar situation at home, I asked him, "Do you have a screwdriver?"

He found one quickly and handed it to me, a bit curious.

I used it in the lock, and in no time, it popped open, and I let Larry out.

The manager looked as relieved as I was. Then he offered me a job in the service department. I liked that guy. He made a huge deposit.

Then there was the rude Heart Breaker who saw me waiting outside the big men's room in the hallway of our doctor's office building. Again, Larry was in there too long, and I knew he was in trouble. I asked the guy heading into the restroom if he could try to help. He looked at me like I was crazy. He went in and did his thing, came out, and walked past me as if I wasn't there. He infuriated me but also made me determined. I walked into the men's bathroom, kicked the stall door as hard as I could, broke the lock, and it slammed open. This scared Larry, but he was free. I felt like Superwoman that day.

A Volunteer

Larry loved to play cribbage, and I didn't. For a long time, his mind allowed him to play and do the counting, but he wasn't up to any cribbage club. Then I found Katelyn through a volunteer placement service. She was such a Heart Warmer! A beautiful young millennial, she was finishing up her bio-engineering degree. She used her ninety minutes between classes at the University of Minnesota to drive over and play cribbage with Larry. Each week, I'd remind Larry that Katelyn was coming to play cribbage with him. He would eagerly haul out the card table, set up the chairs, and get the cards and crib-bage board ready.

Then, full of energy, Katelyn would arrive—truly a breath of fresh air. She would cheerfully greet Larry, ask all about his week, which he never responded to, but it didn't matter to her. They would sit across the table, and he would shuffle and deal the cards. The entire time they "played" cribbage she would talk to him about her plans for spring break, her big adventures, and her classes. She always had photos on her phone to share. If Larry made a mistake with the cards, she ignored it or helped him.

As she was leaving one afternoon, she gleefully said to me, "I asked Larry a question, and he kind of answered it." While this was supposed to be a time I could have for myself, I found her so delightful that I stayed close at hand to hear all the chatter. I actually found myself smil-ing in the other room.

Sometimes I'd bake cookies while she was there so she could take some with her.

My heart is warm just writing this.

Early Care Companions
In order for me to get a break in my week, I hired a com-pany to provide a four-hour companion for Larry. First on the scene were the two "church ladies" who alternated times. I call them this because they were round, older women who read their Bibles while they sat in the room with Larry, who was watching TV. Their sweet tempera-ment and sugary words were lost on him. Sometimes they would play cribbage or a game, but they weren't motivated to do much else. They didn't make a deposit

or a withdrawal because they offered nothing. They asked for a reassignment. I don't think they liked us.

Then there was Bob, who came in sloppy sweatpants and a T-shirt. He was so intimidated that Larry was an attorney that he overdid everything. When I told him that Larry didn't speak, he talked loudly. But worse, he was talking to Larry as he would a child. This was his first job and he really wanted to do it well. My direction to Bob was to keep Larry active, which resulted in him bringing over his favorite DVDs to watch. That wouldn't have been so bad, except that they were nothing that Larry would ever watch. He never thought to ask, "What would Larry like?" Bob's last day was when he brought a package of muffin mix and had Larry making muffins. I came home to see poor Larry filling muffin tins with Bob directing him like he was a two-year-old. Larry caught my eye and looked at me like something was very wrong with this picture. Bob was a Heart Breaker.

I had words with the organization, and they thought Julie would fit the bill. She did.

Julie was the companion for Larry I was looking for. She came with ideas of what she and Larry might do and was always looking for other options. Sometimes they went to see an action movie, which Larry liked, and she didn't. They even volunteered together at Second Harvest Heartland a few times. It didn't matter that Larry was quiet, because she was chatty, and when they were tired and watching CNN, she was always commenting on the news. I think Larry was having his version of fun with Julie. She was a true Heart Warmer because she was doing this work from her heart.

One evening after their "date," Julie wrote telling me that Larry insisted on buying her lunch. "He always likes to be the man," she said.

I remember the sadness in her eyes when she had to tell me that Larry had changed to the point where she could no longer be helpful. She worried that she couldn't keep him safe. We both knew he needed more than a companion. But I didn't want to face it. Even after she was not working for us, she would stop by or call to see how Larry was doing. Julie was a lovely character in this story and an example of a real Heart Warmer.

Larry's Former Client

Virginia called on Christmas Day to invite our family for a traditional Chinese dinner at her restaurant. It seemed very important for her to see "Attorney Larry," as she called him. She was persistent. We don't celebrate Christmas, so we had no plans, but we had out-of-town guests. Virginia said, "Bring them too," which meant the number attending would be twelve.

From the greeting at the restaurant's front door, I knew that Virginia was aware that this wasn't the Larry she once knew, but she never let on. We were seated at a huge round table with a turntable in the middle. Virginia made sure she sat next to Larry. Then she ordered what seemed like every variety of food on the menu.

As the turntable of food floated past us, Virginia leaned into Larry and spoke to him loudly enough for everyone to hear.

"Larry, I closed the big deal we started together a couple of years ago."

Larry's lack of response didn't stop her.

"I cried because you weren't there, and you didn't see it end."

If Larry knew what she told him, it would have been a Heart Warmer, but seeing all the delectable food passing in front of him, he got distracted. He had his chopsticks ready to grab a fried shrimp before it moved out of reach. Seeing this, I hit him under the table, trying to get him to pay attention, but the shrimp was more enticing.

For me, that evening was more of a Heart Breaker. I wish it could have been a real gift to Larry, something he would feel good about. Virginia was letting him know that he was important to her and she missed him. But even if it had no effect on him, the truth is Virginia was a real Heart Warmer. Everyone around the table saw a side of Attorney Larry that they didn't know. It was a meal and an experience to be remembered.

Friends and Family

Lucky for me, I have a best friend, Karen, who is the embodiment of a Heart Warmer. Without any coaching, Karen treated Larry as a human being who was still with us, always accepting and then adapting to where Larry was in his illness or what he seemed to need.

Along with Karen and her husband Lee, we went to Chicago to see *Hamilton*. Larry wasn't at his best at that time, but the trip was almost enjoyable because I knew that Karen would be as protective of Larry as I was. It became one of my fond memories. We were all dressed up, with the guys in suits and Karen and me in lovely outfits, with sensible shoes of course. Looking at us, you'd think everything was normal. I just wish it was.

To this day, Karen calls to check on me almost daily. Her love made my life brighter and truly warmed my heart. She showed me how to be a best friend, which I will always be for her.

There were other Heart Warmers in our life. Larry's brother Stuart and his wife Joann live in another state, as do my sister Lenore and her husband Paul. They were far away, but they never showed Larry that they had given up on him. In fact, his brother would always start our weekly FaceTime visits with a hearty, "How are yuh, Lar?"

Our friend Carol would stroll arm in arm with Larry as we walked to a movie or dinner, talking to him all the way as if nothing had changed.

And of course, there were some friends and even family members who were Heart Breakers and self-selected to stay at a distance. Either they were uncomfortable being around Larry, almost like they were afraid dementia was contagious, or they didn't know what to say or how to be there for us. It was OK. We didn't miss them.

As I became able to distinguish Heart Breakers from Heart Warmers, I learned to manage them, reducing the sting of Heart Breakers and relishing every Heart Warmer. I also learned how to be a Heart Warmer for others.

To minimize Heart Breakers, I had to step up at times, often making hard choices, asking myself, "Do I really care? Do they really matter?" That meant I had to get over being embarrassed about telling people about

Larry's disabilities and let go of people with negative energy. Knowing that people meant well, I tried very hard to forgive and forget if something landed wrong or had a negative impact. I couldn't afford to bankrupt my depleting emotional bank account.

When it came to Heart Warmers, I needed all I could get. Being around them allowed me to relax. Whenever someone was even *trying* to be there for us, I would always express my gratitude and appreciation. It's that old saying, "You attract more bees with honey."

Family

Matters

Matriarch or Martyr

Note to therapist: *Sarah knew I was upset with her when she kept pushing for us to have a "plan" and to "get help." I told her she didn't see what was going on between Larry and me. It's as you've said—she only gets the progression from bad to worse with no upticks along the way. Sometimes it seems like she isn't interested or doesn't have the capacity to hear about what's really happening, so I don't share much.*

Her response: I think that it is unrealistic to think that anyone living outside your house could possibly see or feel what you do.

J'm seventy-five years old, no longer a wife, but still the matriarch of the family, and I want to stay that way. It's the role I love, and I take it very seriously.

When Larry got sick, I believed the family looked to me for guidance, support, and strength. As the matriarch, I wasn't just Larry's protector, but theirs too. I wanted to keep my daughters and their families from hurting by being the strong one.

That didn't last long. I quickly learned I wasn't as strong as I wanted to be. I needed them. Yet learning to turn to them for help without feeling like I was a burden was one of my big challenges, especially since I was confused and unclear of what to even ask for. To make it even worse, sometimes I forgot to say "please" and "thank you."

Moving from matriarch to martyr would have been easy, but that was not an option. Becoming a martyr would turn me into a character that books are written about—the demanding, crabby, overbearing pain in the ass.

Still, as I listened to the stories told by the young women I worked with, where a family member had a dementia diagnosis, the inevitable tension between adult children and parents became very clear to me. Their honest comments revealed a truth that wasn't easy for me to hear.

"I feel so bad, but I just can't be there whenever my mom needs me. I have a family and a business to manage."

"A load is off my shoulders now that I found a memory facility for my parents. It will be good for all of us."

"My brother just took over."

"I'm the one doing everything."

"My sister and I disagree, and Mom always sides with her."

It was as if I had my own research lab that gave me a rare opportunity to get a glimpse into what Eve and Sarah might be thinking and how family dynamics show up during these difficult times.

Even though my colleagues' words sounded harsh, they were spoken out of concern and love for their families. The women were sad, and their hearts were heavy.

While they never saw it, I saw instances where the mother was in the middle of a triangle between her ailing husband and her strong-willed children.

I heard a story from a woman who was very upset about her mother's decision to allow her father living with dementia to complete a birdhouse project using his woodworking tools.

"I told Mom it was too dangerous for him to be using these tools."

Her mother had argued with her, "Why not let him do something he loves?"

The storyteller took a big sigh of exasperation and concluded, "She won't listen to me!"

By far the hardest thing for me to hear was a comment about a "stubborn" mother in a situation like mine. It often came when a young woman would talk about her desire to hire outside help and the mother would resist, creating a struggle between them.

One frustrated woman said that her mom told her, "I need this time to be with your dad. We are doing OK."

It pained me to realize the daughter didn't get it. She wasn't the wife. It made me consider that my daughters didn't know a lot about what went on privately between Larry and me, and we wanted it that way.

A young woman in one of my groups talked about her father who had Alzheimer's and passed away just before Easter. Her comment struck me as she described the feeling of being liberated.

"We had a quiet, peaceful Easter for the first time in many years," she said. "We were together and not worried about whether Dad was doing OK. We weren't thinking constantly about him, his needs, or his safety. It was kind of nice to just be."

I heard a lot.

This is part of the dementia story that we don't like to talk about. Everything, including family relationships, is upended and strained by uncertainty about how to "be." Yes, my daughters' lives changed, but it wasn't the same as the upending I experienced. We all loved Larry in our own way. Without paying attention, there was the potential to put more stress on our family than we needed. We already had enough to deal with.

In our case, most of the stress came from managing expectations, usually mine. When you have strong daughters like I do, especially at a time when none of us knew what to anticipate, disappointments were inevitable. It was important for me to recognize when asking for help could lead to unfulfilled expectations.

Sarah recently told me, "At first we felt like we were constantly disappointing you."

As hard as it was for me to ask for their help, my daughters didn't volunteer assistance immediately. When they didn't see what I thought was obviously a need, or when they said, "Yes, I'll do it, but not today," I felt like they let me down. All of this was made worse by my lack of patience. No one moved to action as quickly as I wanted.

To avoid being disappointed, I found myself making excuses for them or assuming they were too busy. This meant I didn't even try to ask for anything, even though they told me, "If you would just ask, we would do it."

Then my silent response to myself was, "Yes, but when?"

Sounds like a martyr to me.

Asking "Will you do me a favor?" wasn't working either. These were not favors, but part of being in this family. A favor would have been something nice to do, but I had things that needed to be done.

If I was stewing over a request that didn't get the attention I wanted, my temperament would become irritable and the temperature in the house would rise. That's when Larry would hover over me, as if he could soothe my irritation. It was sweet but not helpful. Things needed to change, and it had to begin with me. It was a call for another attitude adjustment.

We found our way when I returned to my role as the family matriarch—the wife, mom, and grandmother they came to expect. I did a lot of self-talk to slow down, take a breath, and then consider the impact of my words and actions. I stopped worrying about asking the girls for help but got better at *how* I asked.

"Will you run to Target?" became, "I'd appreciate it if you could stop at Target for me. When do you think you can?"

If I stated, "Dad is scheduled to volunteer tomorrow, and I can't take him. Can you?" I'd get back, "If you would have told me a few days ago, I might have been able to adjust my day." Instead, I'd make my request as far in advance as possible. We even started a shared online family calendar so everyone knew when things were coming up that might need attention.

Setting realistic expectations for them and for me solved a lot. If it was too much, I knew they would let me know.

Some things worked better than others. Sarah's plan for a regular Tuesday evening meeting to go over the week didn't last more than a month. They seemed to always get cancelled by one of us, usually me. Instead, one or both of the girls started giving me a call each day to check in. It was understood that if I needed a conference call to sort things out, it immediately happened. In an emergency, everyone showed up. It took us a while to get to this point, and it required effort from all of us, but I knew that it was up to me to set the stage.

I had a stark bump into reality when Eve told me, "I miss you. It seems like we are always talking about logistical stuff. I just want my mommy."

I wanted to be her mommy too. We had become focused on "stuff" and not our relationships to each other.

I had to push reset. Something needed to change. If it hadn't, we would never have gotten to where we are today. I had to put as much energy as I could into being the matriarch while still keeping Larry as my top priority. And everyone understood. I wanted to be there for them, and they wanted to be there for me. We just needed to figure out how.

Little did I realize that as I persevered through the months and years, I became a role model for my family. I was who I was and who I had to be. I was so busy living in our world of dementia that I didn't think that others were observing me.

On one of our darkest Mother's Days, I remember Sarah handed me a card and then watched me with great attention as I opened the envelope and read the front panel. It contained a long list of touching affirmations about what was learned from a mother. Inside were Sarah's handwritten words. I could actually feel the emotion she felt when she wrote, *"On this, the strangest of Mother's Days, know that we are surviving with grace because of what you taught us."*

And then there was Nate's bar mitzvah speech which he delivered nine months after Larry's death. The theme of his speech was people doing hard things.

He said, "My Nana is another person I admire because she had to stay with the challenge of taking care of my Papa when he was struggling with dementia. It was a constant pressure, and yet she gave him a normal daily life throughout his struggle. He always sat at his place at the table on Shabbat, he joined us for our summer vacations to the North Shore, even last summer, and he was always at the center of every family gathering, which I know gave him great pleasure—and that's all because of Nana."

I'm glad I was seated when I heard his words.

Courageous Conversations

Excerpts from a letter written to my daughters and their husbands shortly after Larry's diagnosis: I need to keep fighting to hold on to Dad as long as I can. That means figuring out how to create the best life possible with many uncertainties. That fight is taking energy. I don't have the energy to monitor what I say or don't say to you. So here is what I need and ask of you. I need to be real and ask that you understand and question me, without judgment. I need you to accept that sometimes I am fragile, confused, and often sad. I need to advocate for myself without becoming talked about as "SHE"—the one you tiptoe around. I want you to know I will try very hard to be there for you too.

If we don't have this agreement, I fear there will inevitably be hurt and resentment on both sides, which is the last thing we want. I know you can't read my mind, nor me yours; that's why we need to keep talking together.

Let's try to remember that each of us will be impacted by this in our own way.

This short excerpt from a longer letter I wrote to my family says a lot. Through my writing, I allowed myself to be vulnerable because I was desperate to tell the truth in a way that my family would hear. I told it as I felt it. It was an earnest request from my heart—and something I wasn't comfortable doing.

But Larry's diagnoses abruptly disrupted our family's way of being. Expectations were altered, plans became tentative, and relationships were strained. The pending needs of Larry's disease threatened to wear out our entire family system. My daughters were pulled between their own lives and their mother who they once thought was Super Mom but now seemed fragile, and their father who they could always count on but was now dependent on others. Nothing could be taken for granted. There was a lot for all of us to learn. It could no longer be "lean on me" or "lean on Dad," and I didn't want to lean on them—at least not too much.

While we shared the intensity of Larry's diagnosis, we each had our own ways of addressing the feelings surrounding it. Eve was losing "Daddy," and her heart hurt. As an introvert, she held her emotions in her head, often confusing me with her silence. When she did share her sentiments, they were well thought out, but I didn't always understand the reasoning behind them. Her husband, Lawrence, defended Larry whenever he faltered, later realizing he was in denial about the changes in Larry. It was his way of keeping the hurt away.

My triage partner was Sarah. While feeling the losses deeply, her problem-solving gene kicked in, giving her something concrete to manage. Some days she just pointed me in a direction, and I needed that. Aaron, her husband, appeared to take things as they came, but it was just that, an appearance. He endured Larry's sharp-edged teasing directed at him, understanding that it was how Larry showed affection to another guy he cared about. Seeming lighthearted and often funny, Aaron kept his real emotions private until he would hug me, and nothing more needed to be said. Their sons Max, Sam, and Nate were always looking out for Papa's safety. They were our protectors and our joy makers.

Then there was dear Larry, who took his role as the "head of the family" seriously to the end. As long as his family was around him, his life was good, and he was content. Whenever we gathered, he would take attendance to make sure everyone was present. Even in his last years, if someone was missing from the table or in a row at temple, he'd ask where they were. Sometimes we would need to explain for the third or fourth time that "Lawrence is working" or "Max is at school." He was unsettled if all nine of us weren't together. For fun, we took attendance when we were in the car with the boys on the way to some adventure. I'd call out each name, and they would reply "here," including Larry. If all of us were walking in a mall, or even to the beach, Larry was at the end of the line making sure no one in his troop strayed.

For as long as he could, he felt responsible for making sure his family was intact.

We depended on him for that.

As my daughter said, "His job was to launch us into the world and then sit back and watch us with pride."

Even with all the love we had for each other and all the tender moments, my daughters and I had our differences—differences that could create moments of tension. There were times when Eve showed up "just to be with her dad," something she needed, and I would see it as an opportunity to ask for something I needed. Or Sarah would ask for my assistance with the boys without realizing that my energy was spent. I felt guilty saying, "I can't today." And because it seemed like there always was something to do, Sarah and Eve often looked for the most efficient solution, especially when they had other things on their to-do list. That left me without time to process options with anyone, something I was missing without Larry's input.

An observer once told me, "You have a lot of women 'directors' in your family." It was true. We were never short of opinions and solutions. We all had a lot on our minds. We all had a lot to say, and none of us were shy about expressing ourselves—sometimes in loud voices.

There wasn't a lot of listening going on.

In the midst of tense moments and difficult times, we were being tested like never before. Instead of acknowledging the tension, our pattern was to react to it with some fix or another task for someone to do, usually me.

Little time was spent expressing feelings or trying to understand them. The risk of unintentional hurt or clashes was too high. Our patterns needed to be broken.

While uncomfortable and unpolished, the courageous conversations our family started early and revisited often saved us. I call them courageous because they were real expressions of thoughts and feelings. I call them conversations because they were interactive, requiring understanding over judgment, forgiveness over resentment.

We had to learn to talk less and listen more. And sometimes we had to take a breath to think about what was unsaid and why.

Admittedly my consulting experience kicked in as I encouraged us to talk about what was working, what wasn't, and how we were feeling. We had to coach each other to be clear on what we needed. And because we were all moving so quickly, many of these interactions didn't look like a typical "conversation" because they happened as needed or on the fly.

"Eve, these doctors' appointments for Dad are getting too hard for me to do alone. I get emotionally hooked and can't think straight. Will you please come with me? I need you."

Or Sarah saying, "Maahhm"—which is how she said "Mom" when frustrated with me—"What are you really asking here? You are confusing me."

To which I would answer, "Stop yelling at me!"

And in the background, you could hear Aaron saying, "Yeah, Saraaah."

Our real success came when we held a family meeting. Sitting at the dining room table, we struggled together.

And guess who was at his place at the head of that table? Yes, Larry was right there with us. First because that was his place and we were talking about him, and second because we couldn't figure out how to keep him away.

And here is a sad truth. All of this took an abundance of joy from our family interactions. As I look back, we still laughed together, but not as much. We still shared stories about the boys' cute antics or the adults' career achievements, but not as many or as often. We went places and did things together, but there was always a shadow of lost pleasures surrounding us.

We accepted that we were never going to get everything right. Sometimes our conversations were messy. Sometimes emotions got heated. But we got better at taking time to understand the uncertainty each one of us was facing. As a result, our interactions were focused on finding the right balance between asking for what we needed, giving to others when they asked, and then warmly receiving when others delivered. It was a delicate balance. In our hearts, we all knew that Larry could tip the scale at any moment.

The Nana and Papa Team

Note to self: I always knew that being a devoted papa was the legacy Larry wanted to leave behind. Now that he is sick, it's my job to make sure that happens.

*L*arry and I were not just a husband and wife team, we were the Nana and Papa Team, titles we took very seriously. From the minute Max and then his twin brothers, Nate and Sam, were born, the boys were a huge part of our life. Every Friday until they started school was our day with them. Larry's clients all knew not to call on Friday. Our house became our grand-sons' second home, complete with their own bedrooms.

If they were with us, they knew there would be some special "field trip" or activity. Time with them was our sacred time together. To this day we have a rule: "What happens at Nana and Papa's house stays there."

The boys are teens now, and they tell me it's hard for them to remember sitting on the floor racing cars or building long train tracks with Papa. They don't remember the little cars that were always a "surprise" found in Larry's pockets, nor do they remember the trip when they learned how to fish from Papa, who had never fished in his life. Their only memories are those when Larry was changing, not of a sick man, but as a Papa with limitations and still having good times with them. Their last memories are what they are because I knew that Nana was going to keep Papa in their hearts.

It wasn't the Nana and Papa Team leading anymore; it was me taking charge with the boys helping, always alerting me of anything I should know.

Instead of Larry watching over us, we all had to keep a watchful eye on him. I felt bad when I found myself reverting to some of the skills I used when raising small children. But I needed to monitor him, especially when we were in a crowd or in an unfamiliar place. It's probably why he gave me his "leave me alone" look when I'd caution him, especially in front of the boys. He was right. His dignity needed to be maintained, and I had to be conscious about helping him still feel like Papa to the boys he loved. At the same time, I had to keep him safe.

I can remember the winter right after Larry got his diagnosis and we took the boys to the Fire and Ice Festival in our community. It took place on a frozen lake. There were various games on the ice and a little train made from huge plastic buckets, pulled by a small snowplow. On the shore of the lake was a large bonfire for warmth. It was a January tradition with Nana and Papa that only Minnesota families would think was fun.

All bundled for the sub-zero temps, we carefully made our way out on the ice. The boys thought it was really cool—wait, it was really cool, probably -3°F. Of course, if the boys fell, they were so padded with their jackets and snow pants they couldn't get hurt. Larry and I, on the other hand, were not that safe. Standing tense from the cold, a sudden awareness came over me. *This was a crazy idea.* I was no longer a participant but a watchdog. I couldn't tell you how many times I said, "Be careful! Watch out."

Even with all my cautions and heightened attention, we had a great time. I have a cute photo of Larry stuffed into one of those bucket train cars holding Sam tightly. In the photo, Sam is smiling gleefully as Larry looks miserable. But when it came to the boys' enjoyment, Larry was always a good sport.

The best part of attending this event was the satisfaction of having done it together (and having some delicious hot chocolate at the end). Once we got into the car with our red cheeks and frozen noses, I took a big sigh. I felt a sense of fulfillment combined with great relief. The boys never realized how much I was fretting while they were playing. I knew this tradition needed to end. It was too dangerous.

While walking on ice in sub-zero weather is an extreme example, it had become clear that there were things we just couldn't do with the boys anymore.

But there were still things we could do. They just had to be set up differently. Larry had to remain Papa, a role that was such an important part of his identity, and the boys needed to have great memories of him in that role.

One of our wonderful Papa-and-the-boys events came on a day when Nana didn't think she could be a lot of fun. I had little energy to entertain the boys, so I came up with a plan for an activity that I thought might keep all of them busy. I planned to relax.

This was at a time when Larry was beginning to have difficulty forming words, so he said very little. Quiet as he was, if the boys were around, he was nearby, even if he was just watching. It was almost as if he didn't want them to forget him.

Earlier in the week, while cleaning a closet, I discovered Larry's old coin collection. As a youth, he started buying minted proof sets and collecting old coins. He tried to organize them, but mostly they were thrown in a box. We also had a large container of miscellaneous coins. Each night Larry would unload small change from his pocket and throw them in the jar. This was back when people actually used cash.

Hmmm, I thought. What if the boys went through the coins with Larry and he showed them his collection?

It would be good for him, and the boys would learn something about their Papa.

It would also give me some time to sit back and just watch instead of directing.

I brought out the coins and set them out on a table, and they all dug in.

All Sam saw was money. Max was vaguely interested. It was Nate who was into it and impressed by the "ancient" coins from 1970 or earlier. He asked, "Papa, can I keep these?" Larry was delighted that he had something of value to offer and easily agreed that Nate could be the keeper of the coin collection.

But that wasn't the end of it. There was that big jar of loose silver dollars, quarters, nickels, and dimes that were designated as the boys' money. Knowing they didn't want fistfuls of coins, I suggested we take them to the bank, put them in the coin counter, and get paper money.

We divided the coins in three bags, one for each grandson, then headed to the bank and found the coin counting machine. Nate, Sam, and Max gathered around the machine, with Larry right in the middle trying to help. Sam started dumping his coins first. The machine started spinning and then made a grinding noise and stopped. It was stuck.

Larry, always ready to fix things even if he didn't have a clue what to do, immediately stuck his hands in the drum, trying to loosen it. Sam was getting nervous. He looked on in fear that all of his money was lost. A friendly banker came over to help and saw an old silver dollar lodged in the shoot. He gave me an odd look.

"Why would you put these silver coins in the machine anyway? They are worth much more if you take them to a coin dealer."

So much for my quiet day! We were off to a coin dealer with the boys' treasures.

That's when the day turned into not just a scrapbook moment, but a scrapbook day for everyone.

At the office of Rare Coins and Treasures, we were greeted by Pete, a stern looking man, who seemed to be checking us out. I thought we might be in trouble for bringing him young kids carrying little plastic bags of coins. It was not the case at all.

Pete was serious all right, but he made no attempt to minimize his new customers. He escorted us past cases of coins, guns, silver trays, and other assorted treasures to his desk where he seated the boys in big green leather chairs set across from his huge walnut desk. Larry and I were the observers in the back. I had a feeling this was going to be something we wanted to remember so I had my iPhone ready for photos.

This fine man asked the boys to stack the coins by size. First, he took Sam's coins since he could see that Sam was chomping at the bit. Then he moved to Nate, and then Max. One by one, he entered each coin's serial number into his computer to determine its value based on silver content. Sam couldn't hold back his dimpled smile when he learned he had a silver dollar that was worth twenty-one dollars. Pete continued to play it straight.

Looking at them over the top of his glasses, he explained, "You can take the cash out now or hold on to your coins to see if the silver value increases over time."

There was no waiting for these boys. "We will take the cash now."

In the end, each of the boys received checks for around 150 dollars. They were ecstatic—all the way home, they were figuring out how to spend the money.

During this event, Larry sat proudly. I could tell that seeing the boys learn about his coins and then find value in them brought him pleasure. It was part of his story, a small piece of who he once was. Not only did the coins have value, but Larry felt valued. It was a great day for the boys too. They learned about Papa, and they had cash to spend.

It wasn't the day I planned for, but wow! It was wonderful. The interaction, the satisfaction, and the natural flow of events all made Larry feel like king for the day. I had a choice that day. I really wanted to sit with a good book, have the boys play by themselves, and let Larry sit contently and watch TV. It would have been so much easier—and a lost opportunity in so many ways. For me, it was one of those days when I knew I did the right thing as a wife and Nana. I slept well that night.

The boys learned valuable lessons about compassion and caring during their last years with Papa. They were never afraid of him as he changed and always reached out a hand to help him so we could continue to have our adventures as long as we could—adventures that kept Papa with them. They never abandoned him, and he knew it. He was always watching them, absorbing their love and giving it back in the best way he could.

To Larry's delight, all three boys never left our house without kissing and hugging him as they said goodbye. Even in his last days when he was unable to return the gesture, they could feel his love. It wasn't about that moment but a relationship that was intentionally nurtured over time.

Together Fifty Years

Letter to my family: *Weeks ago, I embarked on a project to put a photo book together of the fifty years Dad and I have been married. As I scanned more and more photos, I realized the task was too big and that it was about the process I was going through more than the end project. While it was fun to see all of you at various stages of your life, be reminded of the many travels and trips up north, and see grandsons enter the story, it was the love story of how it began and the early years that kept drawing me back. It took me to our youth and what it felt like to be deeply in love and to believe we had all the time in the world to do all we wanted to do.*

*F*rom the time of Larry's diagnosis, I prayed we would celebrate our fiftieth anniversary together. I made a commitment to myself to find joy at this milestone event. No matter what, there would be love, laughter, celebration, and excellent champagne. This was no fantasy; it would become a reality.

Celebrating in a big way was nothing new for us, especially when it came to major birthdays or anniversaries. Because we were born in the same year, Larry and I celebrated our big birthdays with trips to Alaska, Italy, and Paris. And the two of us had many small private celebrations that were very special. I've always needed to mark these moments, and now I know why. Nothing can be taken for granted.

That's why there was no doubt in my mind that our fiftieth anniversary was going to be something big. It would have been momentous even if Larry were healthy. Without me even knowing it, our fiftieth would be the high point of the love story we were writing. In the following year, he declined rapidly. We barely made it to fifty-one years.

About a year before, I had already begun thinking about what would make this milestone event special. It was almost like good medicine to dream of what the celebration could be. I once read that finding joy is a process. The process of planning this event absolutely brought me joy.

As I came up with great ideas, there was always this voice in the back of my head saying, *Really? Are you crazy?*

I came very close to putting money down on a luxury train trip through the Rocky Mountains. Larry and I talked about seeing Banff many times over the years. I thought this would be perfect as something special. I convinced myself that we could do it. The sales representative said they had lots of experience with older passengers, even those with dementia. She was a great salesperson, letting me know that the travel company offered a large discount for booking early. Still, I was reluctant to give her my credit card.

Then as I was trying to decide what to do, a strong memory popped into my head of an eleven-day cruise we took to the Caribbean. It was the end of the first year of Larry's diagnosis. Everyone we asked told us cruises were easy ways to travel. "You'll have a great experience," they said. It seemed like a good idea at the time, especially since it was in December and the weather was already freezing in Minnesota. A warm getaway was very appealing.

It was not a good time. The stress of going through customs, tracking all the papers we needed, finding our way around the ship, Larry getting pick-pocketed while getting cash at an ATM while in port (which I should have never let him do in the first place), and on and on made me a madwoman. I was constantly on high alert. There was no joy! Actually, I was miserable and couldn't wait to get off the damn ship.

With that experience in mind, I had to face the fact that the Rocky Mountain trip was no longer an option.

I entertained several other ideas only to realize I was fooling myself and probably putting us in danger. If I used my question, "What could go wrong?" the answer always came up, "Lots."

One awareness I've had as I write this is that, while I was planning in my head, I didn't think about the toll these experiences would have on my health. Instead, I spent parts of many sessions with my therapist presenting an idea and then moving right into how I would handle the logistics. I was focused on Larry's physical challenges, not mine. While I was elaborating, she would interject with one of her astute questions that had me pause and face my own limitations. If I was realistic, I should have been asking myself, *Can I do it? What is the cost to me? Would it be joyful for me?*

Determined to find the right way to celebrate, I kept looking. My driving force was the fear that fifty years might be all Larry and I would have together.

While I knew what I wanted, I had to go back to the question "What would Larry want?" It was glaringly obvious. He would want to be with his family—all of us together. He really didn't care where it was. I, on the other hand, still needed to mark the occasion with something memorable. I knew this would be a lasting memory for the entire family. It was big!

My new thinking shifted to making it a family affair. We planned a six-day trip for all of us to San Diego—a place with great memories from past trips. Larry and I took the girls there several times when they were very young because his parents wintered there. We made many trips to San Diego and Coronado by ourselves, including celebrating the turn of the century New Year's Eve at a Y2K formal event. I remember it vividly because the woman sitting at our dinner table had on the same dress as I did.

Once we had grandsons, we talked about taking them to the fabulous San Diego Zoo and spending time on the ocean.

Yes, a family trip to San Diego was the answer—and it was. We wrote a great chapter for our story.

One day before the trip, I wrote a long letter to my family. I've included some of it at the opening of this chapter, but here is another selection.

We are embarking on a big trip tomorrow. I'm excited. And of course, there is a lot to think about with Dad in his current state. Oh, I should also mention that I'm not forty years old anymore, but then you knew that.

Most likely, this will be the last big trip Dad and I take together. For that reason, I want to make the most of it. Let's laugh, play, and most importantly, enjoy the love we have for each other. I know that's my plan.

On the eve of our fiftieth anniversary, we invited a small group of our friends who have meant a lot to us over the years to join us at our temple, where we were blessed by our rabbi. Her blessing was personal, acknowledging the many good years we had and the role models we had been for our family. She commented on the strength I was demonstrating in our challenging times, which I deeply appreciated. Then she praised Larry and me for living by our wedding vows taken fifty years ago. It was the beginning of a great tribute to our years together.

The service was followed by a small champagne toast. We were with our lifelong friends who were always by our side. I thanked all of them publicly with an outpouring of gratitude. There was an emotional toast as my daughters told us how we showed them the way to a beautiful marriage. Then everyone held their glasses aloft for the toast. As I moved to clink my glass with Larry, he looked around, surveying the faces in the room. Then he turned, locked his eyes to mine, which meant whatever he wanted to say was coming from his heart, and with tremendous difficulty said, "I love you."

Moved to tears both of joy and sadness, I was speechless.

It was an amazing and beautiful scrapbook moment.

The next day, all nine of us were waiting at the airport to board the plane to San Diego. Sarah and Eve asked everyone to huddle. Then Sarah opened a big bag and pulled out nine blue jersey hoodies and passed them to all of us to wear. They were printed front and back with "Larry and Myrna's Fiftieth Anniversary."

These were not just cute, but as Sarah told me, "They are our way of keeping track of Dad."

Everyone, including my cool, blue-haired, fifteen-year-old grandson, wore them all over San Diego. Larry was looked after by everyone. He never missed a thing and did very well. I had plenty of eyes on the prize.

We had always planned that the trip's highlight would be an amazing dinner celebration on our last night when we were in a beautiful resort on the water of Coronado Bay. It was also Sarah and Aaron's twentieth anniversary while we were in San Diego. While a significant milestone for them, they graciously stepped aside and let Larry and me take the spotlight. Their day couldn't go without some celebration, however, and our last dinner would be a combined event.

Weeks before we left town, Sarah sent me names and descriptions of restaurant options. As might be expected, the area had many fabulous choices. In the end, like so many times in the past, our grand plans changed. We realized it couldn't be the sophisticated, foodie dinner we originally imagined. We had to go back to "What would Larry want?" He wouldn't care where we were as long as we were together. "What would Mom want?" A place that we could get to easily, without a hassle or any possibility of embarrassment.

The resort we were in had a lovely restaurant that seemed to fit that bill. At six o'clock our little troop, dressed in the special outfits we all packed for that evening, promenaded down the driveway to the restaurant. Larry and I were in the back of the line, of course, watching our beautiful legacy in front of us.

We had a cocktail toast for the two anniversaries on a glorious deck overlooking Coronado Bay. Then we all sat together to enjoy a delicious meal but enjoyed our company more.

I had delivered on the promise I made to myself—there was love, laughter, celebration, and excellent champagne. That scrapbook evening became a cherished memory. Everyone, even our server, knew this was supposed to be a very important evening, and it was.

The last thing to do to preserve this event was a family photo. We were all packed to leave for the airport. Everyone was wearing their blue jerseys. Lawrence set up the camera so we could all be outside with the sparkling water of the bay in our background. I asked everyone to gather around Larry and me.

I needed to talk to everyone, but I was speaking for both of us. Trying to hold it together, I let them know that they were our treasures and how this trip was a dream come true. There was so much in my heart that morning, yet I couldn't get the words out. I didn't have to say much. Everyone knew what was unsaid. The gratitude that we had gotten this far. The knowledge that there would be no more big trips like this with Nana and Papa. We didn't know how many more photos of the nine of us there would be. I managed to talk about the significance of fifty years and the love that their dad and I shared.

"My wish for all of you is that you celebrate fifty years with the one you love."

I spoke to the boys. "I know you will have many more big trips with your own families. What I ask is that you hold this one as a special memory of the great times we all had together."

The photo was taken. In the center is Larry, working very hard to smile, and all of us clinging to each other.

Fifty years. We made it.

It's

Complicated

The Relativity of Time

Note to therapist: I know I can't predict the future, but why do I feel forever behind?

Her response: Your note suggests you might need to slow down, breathe, and not be on the edge of your seat. I do not think your pace is sustainable.

Making it to fifty years was a huge milestone and a major accomplishment driven by perseverance and my overwhelming fear of losing Larry before I was ready. But would I ever be ready? That dreaded thought would send me to a depressing place. The loving relationship we had built was being threatened by never knowing how long we would have together. For something that seems so exacting as the four digits for telling time, facing the three progressive diseases that Larry was dealing with made our time together even more precious. The problem was I never knew if I needed to hurry or slow down.

That meant I had to enter a different relationship with time. This wasn't easy for an impatient person who likes to control things, especially when a clock was ticking away my life.

Anyone living with someone diagnosed with dementia or a chronic illness understands the things you once counted on will be gone at some point. Time together will run out. For me that made everything urgent. I turned needs into urgencies that couldn't wait. *I need the earliest date I can get for a doctor's appointment. Anything I order has to be delivered as soon as possible.* Sometimes that was true, but most of the time my struggle to get ahead of Larry's disease pushed me to become a nutcase.

At one point his shoes were too hard for him to just slip into without help. Thinking he needed an alternative, I ran out and bought a similar pair two sizes bigger. The shoes were constantly slipping off, so he shuffled along like Tim Conway when he played an old man. He couldn't walk in them. We went back to me assisting by using a long shoehorn with his old shoes. It was an urgent attempt that failed.

Every problem became an urgent need for a solution, and as soon as I thought I'd solved a problem, something would change. It was like playing Whack-a-Mole. You'd hit one problem, and another would pop up. I looked for moments, never days, when I could relax and let my guard down a bit. Nothing could be predicted, and as Larry declined, time became my enemy.

Making the distinction between urgent and important was hard for me and required many conversations with my therapist. I have limited patience to wait for the "right time." My daughters always got their gifts before Chanukah because I was so excited about them, I couldn't wait. Then I had to buy more gifts for the eight nights that followed.

I was reminded in therapy that if everything was perceived as urgent, I'd miss seeing the special scrapbook moments. The important things needed to prevail. Most of the time, that meant slowing down, which seemed counterintuitive when time with Larry was fleeting.

If you've ever had trouble falling asleep, you know it's worse if you keep checking the clock. Anxiety builds as you attempt to roll over and relax, only making things worse. You start calculating hours until morning or how much sleep you've lost. Ultimately you are a wreck when you do get out of bed. One remedy is to cover the clock.

If you can't go back, and you can't count on one day being like the next, the only thing left is to take each day as a new one. Sure, there were things I could be pretty certain of. Larry would need assistance, he couldn't be counted on for remembering, and on and on. Hours of my time were spent problem-solving and calculating. Just like watching the clock when I couldn't sleep, my anxiety led to frustration—often making me irritable—and frequently resulting in grief. It was taking a toll on me. The sleepless nights were adding up.

I had to cover the clock.

I had to stop asking, "Will we have enough time to . . .?" and start asking myself, "How can I make today a good one—for me, for Larry, *and* for both of us together?" And if I am honest, sometimes I asked, "Will today ever end?"

Oprah Winfrey calls this "living fully present."

Future planning didn't stop, it just needed to be more realistic. There were more plans for today than tomorrow. I needed to learn how to be even more adaptable than ever, always considering what Larry could tolerate and what I could handle. That changed daily.

A big *aha* came when I accepted that not every day needed a plan. That wasn't easy for either of us. Every day in the early years, Larry would ask, "What are we doing today?" and I would have an answer. We always had to be doing something. As long as he was with me, he never complained when there was one more stop, one more thing to buy, one more task before we could rest.

But it was becoming obvious I was wearing him out. I was also wearing myself out. I worked so hard preparing for the race that I was exhausted when the race actually began, and so was Larry.

Once I accepted yet another reality of dementia, I lightened his load, which meant lightening mine. That resulted in a change in our daily pace. While this all makes perfect sense, it was frustrating to think I had to slow down! The reality was that my bandwidth wasn't what it used to be.

On one of those days, when I complained to my therapist about all the things that I was trying to do to keep

Larry active—all the running to museums and movies that didn't seem to amuse him at all, she had an obvious response.

"Sometimes doing nothing is the right thing to do."

That insight led to more and more hours of just being together quietly, something that was good for both of us. Doing nothing was typically very uncomfortable for me. I don't just sit. Yet it felt lovely to know that we were just being together in the same space of our home.

Around dinner time most days, I found comfort knowing Larry was sitting contently in the other room, watching Wolf Blitzer on CNN, while I was in the kitchen cooking. I wasn't fretting over which restaurant to go to for dinner, knowing I would be nervous, watching every move Larry made, hoping we would get through the meal with some satisfaction.

Many afternoons, we'd be in the sun-filled family room, me working on my laptop, and him sitting nearby. I'd turn my head and see Larry sitting there, wearing his reading glasses, face in one of his mystery books as he had done for years and years. Now I was looking at him in that familiar position, except this time, the pages of his book never turned.

Instead of racing in circles trying to keep up our old routines, I had become conscious about pausing and in some cases just stopping. Living with Larry's dementia required a reorganization of our days to get the "busyness" out and allow time to focus on what was important—time together. It was a welcome and needed change.

I link time with courage. It took courage to be comfortable with the fact that time cannot be controlled with progressive illnesses. I had to move from a sense of urgency to a sense of significance. It took courage for me to stare down the clock and allow life to move at its own pace. Had I not done this, had I not focused on the things that would enhance the quality of the time we actually had together, I could have missed that last dance.

Expect the Unexpected

Note to self: We had a wonderful day trip along the Minnesota Valley Scenic Drive. We made several stops at state parks and Minnesota's largest candy store. I packed overnight supplies in case we were having so much fun we could stay overnight in a cute little hotel. We did NOT. When we came home and pulled into the driveway, I thanked Larry for a wonderful day. He replied, "No, thanks for two wonderful days."

Over the years of living through dementia with Larry, I continued to be amazed at what he could still do while not being able to do other things. I never knew what to expect.

Two years after his diagnosis, Larry reminded me that there may be holes in his memory, but there still was wisdom. The reminder came as I was preparing all the numbers for the tax season. We sold his office condo the previous year, and I needed the amount of deed tax we paid in order to figure out the original purchase price. To locate that number required knowing the property identification code. Larry, being a real estate attorney all of his career, would have found this an easy problem to solve. I asked him for his help, and he would sit at his computer searching for who knows what, but after weeks of no answer and seeing his frustration, I knew it was hopeless to think he would find the needed information. I stepped in and learned that we had to go to the county courthouse to get the information.

Determined to resolve this, we got dressed for business and drove downtown. We began at a nice restaurant for lunch, and with that, our errand became an outing. Then we proceeded to the courthouse.

Once inside, it was familiar territory for Larry as he headed straight to the property desk with no confusion. He was in his element. I just followed him.

A smiling clerk with long dreadlocks and a salt-and-pepper beard looked up at me from behind the desk and said the words I needed to hear. "How can I help you?" I explained what I needed.

He asked for Larry's name and, within two minutes, gave us the amount of deed tax we were looking for.

Then to my total disbelief, Larry said to him, "So I just multiply that by one point six five and double it to get the purchase price."

The clerk said, "Yup."

But he wasn't finished. He looked at Larry and asked, "I once knew an excellent real estate attorney who came to the property desk when it was upstairs. Are there other lawyers with your last name?"

Larry answered, "That was me. I retired at seventy."

This awesome clerk stood up with a big grin on his face, reached out to shake Larry's hand, and said, "Congratulations. I'll never make it that long."

Larry walked out of the courthouse as if it was a normal day in the life of Attorney Larry.

I was blown over. I came home and called my daughters and told them this story, ending with, "Some days I don't know which foot to put in front of the other."

When I talked to my therapist about this, she cautioned me, "Just because he impressed you then, doesn't mean this is the new norm."

Which, of course, I desperately wanted to believe.

"Likewise," she said, "when something disappointing happens and breaks your heart, it's not a sign of a swift decline." She coached me to think of these as blips, in other words, not to get too hopeful nor too disappointed. I needed to stay centered, which means I needed to expect the unexpected.

But I still thought I could count on a few things being predictable because I'd seen Larry do them over and over—like making his daily coffee. It sounds ludicrous to use this as an example, but a Keurig coffee maker became a source of unexpected stress. In fact, I blathered about this for an entire therapy session.

Here is how it percolated (sorry, my family likes puns). Larry made coffee every day for over forty-six years in his office, and it was his morning routine to make the coffee at home. Because he liked regular coffee, and I like decaf, keeping this straight was too confusing with his dementia. I didn't want to take this job away from him, so the solution was a Keurig coffee maker that used individual K-Cups. Larry had a small Keurig in his office and knew how to use it, so I purchased the best model available. It seemed like a no-brainer.

Not so. If you didn't clean this particular model every week, it overflowed. Cleaning didn't always work, so Larry would just stand and watch the pot overflow. I called the company and said it was defective, and they sent another. Larry made coffee for three or four days, and then it plugged up and the counter would overflow again. I called the company and complained once more. Another similar coffee maker was sent. It was the only solution they offered. I know it sounds unbelievable, but we just couldn't get that model to work without flooding. It might have been us, or our water, or who knows.

That left me with a husband who was still able to make coffee, wanted to do it, but couldn't.

I called the company again, but this time I pleaded using the big D word, "Please send me another model. My husband has dementia, and he needs something that is easy for him to use. We don't need a fancy model. Can you send a replacement? I don't care if it's cheaper. All I want is one that is basic and user friendly." I intensified the pleading with lots of emotion in my voice, and said, "I just want him to be able to make his own cup of coffee, dammit!"

The poor woman had no further questions. She sent me a basic unit.

I had two choices: throw the coffee maker out, which would mean Larry would not be able to do something he was used to doing for years, or take charge with my own solution.

As I revisit this story, it's clear that this wasn't about coffee or a coffee maker. It was about keeping Larry independent. He needed to keep making his coffee. We both expected him to be able to do it, and it was something he could still do and feel good about doing. While this episode infuriated me, I'm happy to say that Larry continued to make his coffee daily, even though at the end, that cup of coffee just sat untouched on the table.

I had to remember that Larry wanted to stay in the game of living. When he was disappointed in himself or when he thought he disappointed me, I could see the embarrassment and sometimes fear in his eyes.

Living through dementia was like a roller coaster ride at times. The only thing you could really predict was that things would be unpredictable. Our new norm after Larry's diagnosis was a shifting definition of what Larry could and couldn't still do. My job was to keep from seeing the extremes and getting high expectations or huge disappointments.

The Lens of Loss

Note to therapist: There is no lost and then found in our life now. It's lost and still lost. It's getting harder and harder to find joy.

Her response: Some of the happiest people I know in difficult times like yours find contentment by watching a cardinal sing, smelling freshly mowed grass, or simply holding hands.

J often think about an activity I had people in my training class do. The participants who wore eyeglasses switched them with another person and then were instructed to do various activities as they moved around the room. It lasted for three minutes.

There were always some who didn't want to play the "game," certain that they wouldn't be able to see something terrible ahead. They just sat in place uncomfortably waiting till they could get their own eyeglasses back and see things clearly.

After the activity, I asked participants how it felt to see through the lens they were given. They described how things were blurry for them. They couldn't focus and only thought about what they couldn't see. Some said they were disoriented. Others feared for their safety.

The activity was designed to illustrate how we all see things through our own set of lenses. If the lenses are changed, what we see gets distorted and we are thrown off course.

That's how I felt so often when I saw the changes in my life through the lens of loss.

The more I saw pieces of my life disappear, the more my anxiety escalated in anticipation of what "could" be next. This concept is called an amygdala hijack. It is the emotional response from a perceived threat—in my case anticipating another loss—that causes the part of the brain called the amygdala to release hormones that produce an intense reaction that may be out of proportion to the situation. In other words, I was having an oversized reaction to even the smallest loss. As my daughters would say, "Mom, you are catastrophizing again."

A few examples come to mind. In the first, Larry lost his jacket. After searching and searching for it, I bought him an exact replacement, thinking this would just be another episode in our lives. It wasn't. I went crazy worrying about him losing his jacket again. I feverishly wrote his name in everything I could, certain he couldn't keep track of anything. Then when he lost his gloves or his sunglasses, my brain got hijacked with an emotional memory associated with the original loss of his jacket, and I spun off balance.

Another example came one evening when we were having dinner. As we sat together, I glanced at Larry and for some reason noticed his hands.

"Oh my gosh, Larry! Where is your wedding ring?"

He looked down, then held out his hand to show me it was gone.

His wedding ring was missing, and clearly he had no idea where it was.

"What happened to it? We have to find it!" I was hysterical.

My brain got hijacked. I knew better than to go off like that, but I couldn't keep myself from making it into a symbolic event signaling that our marriage was over.

I know it made no sense, but everywhere I turned, there was one form of loss after another—all adding up to tremendous despair. Still, I had blown this one out of proportion.

I remember trying so hard to calm myself down while trying to manage my tone and hide my thoughts and feelings from Larry.

It didn't work.

He knew how upset I was, and he was feeling bad, which only agitated him.

I saw him going through his jean pockets over and over, only to come up without his ring. Then he looked at me like he was a child who had done something wrong.

Of course, this made me feel horrible.

The ring was gone for days. I don't know how many times I went through his pockets—jeans, shirt, jacket. If his underwear had pockets, I would have searched there too.

I was about to give up and attribute it to another disturbing loss, like when his phone disappeared or when his iPad was left on a plane. Each time, I asked myself, "Why would I get him a new one when it will just get lost?" Then I'd replace it.

But losing his wedding ring was different. It was a loss that I couldn't bear at that time. There were too many little things we were losing that were adding up to what I saw as an unmanageable existence.

Then out of the blue, Larry walked over to me, raised his hand to my face, and showed that his wedding ring was on his ring finger.

I was stunned and screamed with amazement.

"You found it! Oh, thank goodness!"

To see my elation brought a delightful sparkle to his eyes—something I hadn't seen before. He didn't want to disappoint me.

I kept asking, "Where did you find it? How did you find it?"

He couldn't answer, but he walked upstairs as I followed him. Then he showed me that he had found it on the floor of the closet where it landed after it fell out of his pants pocket.

I can't explain how he saw it there.

What I do know is that he hadn't done anything out of the ordinary for this to happen. He put it in his pocket when he volunteered at Second Harvest Heartland just like he always did. Then he forgot to put it back on his finger when he was done with his shift. When he hung up his pants that evening, it must have fallen out. It wasn't lost!

This became a scrapbook moment with a happy ending. I'm not sure what would have resulted from a different ending. It's no wonder that one of the first things I did after Larry died was to have his wedding ring sized for my hand. It won't be lost again.

Of course, there were going to be losses and the accompanying sadness, but the impact on me was made worse because with each loss came a dose of grief.

Rabbi Steve Leder, author of *The Beauty of What Remains*, writes about the cumulative effect of grief that comes from experiencing continuous loss. In his book he writes about watching his father live with Alzheimer's for over ten years.

"I used up 60 percent of my grief before my father died," he said.

But if I saw every loss as the end of the world, I could miss the beautiful moments I still had with Larry.

Refocusing became necessary—not easy, but necessary. First, I had to recognize what was happening to me, what I was feeling, and what was triggering my emotions. Then I had to practice mindfulness and stay in the present, letting go of the pain from the past.

I had to shift my focus, change my lens, and sometimes turn from a loss to a pleasant memory.

One of the more difficult losses for the two of us came when I had to move from the warm bed I shared with

Larry to another room to sleep. I felt the sting every night as I walked out of our room down the hall to a cold lonely bed. But I needed rest, and it was becoming too hard to share the bed as his condition worsened. I could see Larry's sad eyes as I kissed him goodnight and turned to walk away.

Leaving him didn't feel right. I had months of restless sleep. All I thought of was the loss of Larry next to me. Then one day I got an idea that helped change my lens and stopped me from feeling sorry for myself. Well, almost.

With the help of Eve and Sarah, we transformed what had now become my bedroom into my serenity room.

We emptied the old furniture, had it painted in a calming color, and bought a comfortable bed, new tables, and a chair. We found soft colored linens and added some charming lamps. It was just for me. To my delight, the room became more than a place to sleep, but also a place to escape when the stress in the house became too much. Very important to this room was that it had a door, which helped me block out the world for a short period of time.

And here is where gratitude came in. The best item I added to the space was a giant canvas print of Monet's water lilies. I love his paintings. Whenever we were in Chicago, the Art Institute was one of my first stops. I'd head to the impressionist gallery and find Monet's lilies.

When I left Larry at night and laid my head on the pillow in my serenity room, I would focus on the print. Shifting the focus transported me to a wonderful time when Larry and I were in Paris and took a side trip to

Giverny, the town where Monet lived and worked amidst beautiful gardens.

Yes, I was missing Larry, but my mind quieted as I began remembering the two of us standing on the small bridge holding hands and gazing at the pond of lilies that Monet painted so magnificently. My wall size canvas allowed me to refocus from loss to a happier time.

While I was experiencing grief and despair over our combined losses, Larry saw his reality. I'm certain there were times when he was embarrassed or sad, but I never thought he dwelled on what he was losing.

This was no surprise. Larry lived with dementia the way he lived his life—a contented man who accepted reality as it came. If things were hard, he found a way to adjust, often making it better. He was never a complainer, and living with me, he should have had lots to complain about. Instead of focusing on what he was losing, Larry chose to focus on gratitude.

This was demonstrated in a short note he wrote about two years after his diagnosis. We took a trip with our grandsons to Washington, D.C. My sister Lenore and her husband, Paul, live there, so we stayed in their home.

The evening before we were going to leave, we all wrote thank you notes to our hosts. Here is Larry's. He was never a good speller, but observe his awareness of loss as he describes his "failing mind." Then he turns to the man he always was.

Translation:
Lenore and Paul, I love being with you and love that you put up with my failing mind. I love our trip and attention to every detail. Love, Larry

Dementia is a condition that keeps taking. From the onset of Larry's diseases, and for the next five years, our marriage experienced loss after loss, until the big loss of losing him.

"I feel cheated," I told my therapist.

"Nothing can prepare you entirely for the loss you feel," she offered. "However, if all you see is the darkness of loss, it *can* be devastating. But staying in that devastation can only add to your sense of pity and apathy."

She was right. I had to stop watching myself lose things.

It took a lot of self-talk, especially as time went on, to remember to stop seeing catastrophes and start seeing realities. Rather than seeing a lost ring, I needed to see a man who would do anything to find it and make me happy. I needed to learn from Larry that amidst the losses there was still gratitude to be found.

That is 20/20 vision.

Where Are You Taking Me?

Note to self: All I can say is that I live a crazy life with a shadow that looks like Larry. If I turn quickly, I may knock him to the floor.

When Larry's questions turned from "Where are we going?" to "Where are you taking me?" I understood that something had shifted in his mind. He had accepted that his independence was diminishing. Decisions about his life and well-being were being made for him, rather than with him. Even knowing his basic personality of accepting what was instead of grieving what was missing, I felt his unhappiness.

"Whatever she says," became his answer to any question when he could speak. When he couldn't speak, he would just look at me.

It was predictable and sometimes brought others a smile, but underneath I knew he was probably experiencing tremendous anxiety.

I can't imagine how frightening it must have been for him to feel captive. He was a man who was so independent, and now he was losing his autonomy, his sense of security, and his dignity. Watching him withdraw and yield told me he was moving to resignation. As his condition worsened, he really had no choice. I became his lifeline for everything. Someone described it as if he were tethered to my side. When I would leave, he would ask when I would return. When I returned, he would seem lighter. I was his stability, his anchor, his beloved.

Transferring his trust to in-home care providers didn't come easily. He wanted me, and I needed space from him to renew and return a better partner for him. It was complex.

Even knowing he had changed, Larry remained a stubborn guy. He kept shaving with a razor because he never used an electric one and made it clear he wouldn't try. Because he was going to do whatever he could, for as long as he could, he hated when we got to the point where I had to shave him.

Whenever possible he helped me help him. Plus, I always assumed he could do things until he proved he couldn't.

As the one he trusted most, I had to understand his vulnerability and take a step back before I acted for my own convenience. It was important to find ways to allow him to maintain his dignity, even when he could no longer control what was happening to his body and his life. If he truly felt captive, our relationship would suffer. I would become his keeper, not his wife. It took a new set of behaviors for me to address his need for emotional security while providing him a sense of autonomy.

"We are together."

"You are safe."

"It's OK."

"Let's try it."

At the same time, while not proud to admit it, selfishly, I needed things to appear right to avoid my own embarrassment or discomfort with his limitations.

When it came to Larry's incontinence, I was tested to my limits. I think my mother is to blame for this. Aren't mothers to blame for everything? She never talked about gross stuff—my words, not hers—and she saw germs everywhere. That's probably why my therapist said I had an allergy to bodily fluids of any kind. It wasn't a problem with my babies or grandsons, but diapers for my husband were hard to face.

It was a huge concession for Larry too. Not only was it a loss of body function, but Larry was a modest guy. I needed to be respectful of this.

He had many accidents before I was willing to accept his new loss. When this happened, he would look helplessly at me, and it would break my heart. We both had a miserable problem, made worse by my discomfort. He needed me to handle something he didn't want me to handle.

After many Google searches for advice and suggested solutions, I was better able to manage the situation but not the emotions I was feeling.

Unpleasant situations still occurred, and hard as it was, I had to remind myself that he couldn't help himself. It was the diseases.

The biggest thing I had to manage was my tendency to sigh deeply, throw my head, and mutter, "I can't believe this is happening." This was not helpful, and I knew it.

And no matter how prepared I thought I was when we went out and about, there always were events I hadn't expected.

One scene I will never forget was a horrific moment in the Costco parking lot. We were heading to the car, and Larry was pushing the cart filled with stuff. I got ahead of him to open the trunk. When I turned around, I couldn't believe my eyes. There he was, walking to the car as his pants were falling below his knees. He didn't seem to be aware of it, or if he was, he had no idea what to do.

It was an "oh shit" moment that caught me off guard. I had to think fast and avoid embarrassing him by screaming at him or running to him. As hard as it was to figure out what to do, I had to think, *Preserve his dignity*. I was the one embarrassed, not him.

He just kept pushing that damn cart until I physically grabbed him and steered him between two parked cars to handle the situation. This was the height of indignity for Larry, if he actually knew what was happening. For me it was disastrous. My recovery from that afternoon took a while.

Once I realized his pants were falling down because he had gotten so thin that his jeans were too big, we took a trip to Macy's to buy some better fitting ones. I had no idea that men's jeans came in low rise, regular fit, boot cut, ripped, washed out, and on and on. All I knew was I wanted to find jeans that fit right and didn't look like work jeans. I had no idea where to start or what size to get because Larry always bought his own jeans and then wore them forever.

This wasn't like buying him a good-looking shirt or sweater "just because." No, this was serious. It was now up to me to dress him.

There was no one to help in Macy's because there never is. I pulled a bunch of styles and sizes and sent Larry to try them on in the fitting room. Then I waited impatiently for him to come out and show me how they looked. That was not a good idea. In fact, it was a terrible experience for both of us. I don't think I need to explain.

After that, I purchased several styles of jeans, brought them home, helped him try them on, realized they weren't right, and then took them back. It became too frustrating to continue.

On a whim, we went to Nordstrom to see if we could find the right jeans. A young guy was eager to help us. I explained the situation, and he looked at me in a manner that let me know he totally understood. I bet he had a grandfather in a similar situation. He asked if I would like to go in the fitting room with Larry and gave us two pairs that he recommended. Both were perfect!

This isn't a commercial for Nordstrom, but we walked out of there with two expensive pairs of jeans that fit and looked great. I'm not sure if Larry really cared at this point, but I knew he always liked to look good. Of course, I was thrilled with our purchase.

This episode wasn't just to find the right jeans. In my mind, it was much bigger. I was letting Larry know that he was important, special, and worth the effort. I hope he knew this.

Yes, it was exceedingly challenging at times. I often said I needed two brains—his and mine—to think ahead and avoid unwanted situations. Larry was quick!

As his abilities became more and more limited, I tried hard not to shame him. It was so hard to read Larry's emotions since his face showed so little, but I could tell that shame was one he still felt. It was as if his shame made him frightened of what he had become. At these tense times my voice tone needed to be calming. When I saw he was upset, and more likely when I was upset, I'd rub his back or kiss his cheek. When I got agitated, Larry would too.

Needless to say, I was seeing dramatic changes in Larry's condition that could not be ignored. Our life was becoming increasingly difficult, and Larry wasn't the only one frightened.

Running

Out

of

Time

Relief

Note to therapist: I think I have enough energy to go one more round. I will hear what the doctor says next week. Then I'm done. I'm finally ready to accept that there is nothing more I can do. Now it's time to make these days count more than ever.

Her response: Two words come up here over and over: ready and relief. Are you ready and relieved?

J've come to the most difficult part of the story to write about. The last year of Larry's life added more conflict, turmoil, and emotional upheaval. I could see the end was near, and I was consumed with dread.

Sleepless nights from worry and an injured knee had gotten me down.

I heard myself saying out loud, "I'm not sure I can do this anymore!"

I was right—there was too much I could no longer do. We were at a point where Larry's needs were more than I could handle. It was evident that a skilled person to assist with Larry's care and do some light housework was imperative—someone who could help me.

Yet I hesitated, questioning myself. *Am I giving up? Have I lost the battle? How can I preserve my relationship with Larry if there are other people caring for him?* No matter what the answers were, I was unsettled knowing I could not keep up this pace and survive.

Once again, I had to look in the mirror and have an honest conversation. I knew what the answer would be.

You know you are in need of help. Now figure out how to make it happen!

And I did.

With this determination began a constant parade of people coming in and out of my house—all there to provide help.

Little did they know how difficult that was on me. Little did they understand how their presence kept me at a distance from Larry. While I needed them desperately, Larry and I had little privacy. After all my effort to keep us close, having them between us didn't feel right. Every moment with him had become more precious.

But I had no choice. I had to have relief.

At first, I was convinced that all I needed was eight hours a week to care for Larry and complete tasks that would give me a break. Once again, I was dreaming.

When I found the right person, it was apparent how stubborn I was. Those eight hours quickly increased, and so did the checks I wrote. It was money well spent.

Let me back up. It's not easy finding the right person for this job. There were two factors at work for me. First, I went into the search with a heavy heart and lots of trepidation. In my mind, there was no one whom I could trust. I feared I would experience incompetence. Second, I didn't even know where to look.

I got a few recommendations from friends who knew of someone who knew of someone. But I am hard to please, especially after my previous experiences with help. I didn't want to use personal connections and then have to explain why I didn't select their referrals.

Since she'd found the service to be reliable, Sarah suggested I try the website referral service she used to hire nannies for her babies. They screen their providers and do background checks, so I followed her suggestion.

With a simple search, I identified four or five providers to screen over the phone. Using interview techniques from my days in business, I put some structure to this troubling process. First, there was a phone conversation with general questions designed to determine if I should even spend more time talking to them.

- *How long have you been doing home care?*
- *What brought you to this type of work?*

- *Describe some of your clients. Have you worked with men?*
- *Where do you live?*
- *What is your experience with dementia?*
- *Do you have any licensure or certificates for caregiving?*
- *What is your hourly rate?*
- *Do you have a minimum number of hours?*
- *Will you work part-time?*

The answers I got from these screening questions resulted in me asking to meet face-to-face with two possible candidates. I wanted to see if there was a connection before I even brought Larry into the picture, so I set up meetings in a coffee shop.

It was winter in Minnesota; there was lots of snow and ice on the street on the day I was set to meet one of the candidates. Hours before our set time, the candidate called to reschedule our appointment. She said she lived a distance from me and feared driving in these weather conditions.

Red flag! One of my hot buttons is people who don't show up on time, every time. If she had a long drive, she couldn't be depended on.

I was down to one prospect.

And then, on another very snowy morning, I met Pauline, a beautiful African woman with a serious yet pleasant demeanor. Everything about her said she was a professional. As she talked about her experience, there was a twinkle in her eye and an occasional tear of empathy. It was clear to me that her heart was into this difficult work.

The interview with Pauline was a conversation where I wove in a list of questions that revealed what I wanted to hear. As I listened, my gut said this could be the person, and I could feel my shoulders relax. I believed she knew what I needed and could provide it.

As we chatted, Pauline told me how she handled difficult situations, and I was able to assess her capabilities. We talked about what made her job easy or hard, and most importantly, where her heart was.

Here are the questions that guided me through that very important conversation.

- *Tell me about your most recent client.*
- *How does your training or past experience make you good at what you do?*
- *Describe an experience with a client that was really hard for you. What made it challenging? How did you handle it? How did you feel?*
- *[Insert situation] happened with Larry, and I didn't know what to do. How would you have prevented this situation from happening? If it happened to you, what would you do?*
- *If you leave a day of work and say to yourself, "That was a good day," what made it good? If it was a "hard day," what made it hard?*
- *Tell me about you. What do you do to relax? What do you do for fun?*
- *What other types of work have you done over the years?*
- *We are Jewish and do not want religious conversations or prayers. How do you feel about that?*

- *From what you know about Larry's condition, what questions or concerns do you have?*
- *Here is what I need from you to work together. What do you need from me?*
- *How can you make my life easier?*
- *How can you enhance the quality of life for Larry, even with his declining health?*

I wish I had asked, "How experienced are you with end-of-life care?"

From the conversations that resulted from these questions, I detected many things that impressed me. Pauline was from Ghana, a culture that respects older people. Because her family was far away, she chose to work in a field where she could care for other families.

I could feel her loving heart as she spoke about her past clients. While led by her compassion, Pauline was a businesswoman, something I appreciated. Days later, she told me, "I'm very fussy about who I will work for."

Apparently, she was interviewing me while I was interviewing her.

Not only would I learn a lot from Pauline, the thought of having someone do light housework and laundry was very exciting. When she said she would take care of both of us by making my life easier and providing whatever Larry needed, I was sold.

I could see relief ahead. I would be able to spend time as Larry's wife in those precious last days.

The next step was for her to meet Larry. That couldn't have gone better.

First of all, she is stunning, and while not a job requirement, I could tell she got Larry's attention. I remember how dull and dreary I felt as he looked her over.

Positive energy surrounded Pauline. Nothing about her gave off sadness or pity. She brought hope with her help, caring with her care.

From the minute Pauline walked into our house, she was part of our lives. And because she had never met either of us before, she didn't experience any loss or despair—until the very end. It was when Larry really took a turn that she told me he had become a father figure for her. While she tried to hide it, I could see that watching him change became hard on her.

I observed Pauline work with Larry and often thought that what was daunting to me seemed effortless to her.

Using a no-nonsense voice, she would say, "Larry, let's put your shoes on now," or, "Larry, it's time to use the bathroom."

Without hesitation, he would follow her directions. Then they would run errands or go out for breakfast or lunch. Nothing seemed to faze her.

One morning I couldn't get Larry out of bed. His eyes fought me as he pulled up the covers in defiance. Then Pauline arrived and walked into the bedroom. She went up to his bed, looked him in the eyes, and said, "Let's get going, Larry. We have things to do."

He immediately cooperated, allowing her to help him out of bed. Then he went right to his dresser to get his shirt so he could get ready to go with her.

She was far more exciting to Larry than I was. If I didn't know better, I would have been jealous.

Finding the right person to bring into our lives came just in time. It is high on the list for what saved my life as Larry was losing his.

As an employer for years, I know that if you treat your employees well, they will return that to you. Pauline knew that she was appreciated. On the other hand, I had to remember that she worked for me. That was a challenge at times because Pauline was a force to be dealt with. Not a complaint, but it was easy to move over and let her take charge. But it was my house and my husband. That meant I had to be clear with directions and express my desires. As a result, we had a very good working relationship.

Pauline started in February, and through April things moved along smoothly. Larry and Pauline did their thing. She would find any reason for them to get out of the house. He loved to ride in her car and listen to her music. Some days, I thought she was a better woman than me. How did she schlep him to the fabric store, Home Depot, and miles away for her favorite Indian food? It wasn't my worry, and I liked it that way.

I was able to work, shop, meet friends, and come home to a content husband and a neat kitchen. Thanks to Pauline, for the first time ever, my underwear was folded neatly and placed in straight rows in my drawer.

I'm reminded of this daily now when I open my drawer to a mess.

It was so great to have someone to talk to at home and to feel supported by someone who saw the daily challenges. From Pauline, I learned how to handle Larry's needs more efficiently without harming my body. Using her serious tone, she would call me over to learn from her. Other times, she would stay in the background, allowing Larry and me to have our private, sacred time. And on those rare occasions when there was nothing to do, Pauline and I would have conversations about life and blessings.

Some days she was the cheerleader I needed. I only wish it would have lasted longer.

Time for Hospice?
Really?

Note to Self: *I read the book that was given to me by the hospice team and had a meltdown. The first paragraph on page seven states that hospice is for those "whose life expectancy is weeks or months rather than years if the illness progresses as expected." Am I jumping the gun with Larry? Is it too soon to face the ultimate end? I want to keep him going, doing, and being. I know this isn't going to get better, but I'm a fighter, and this feels very fatalistic. Am I letting Larry live until he dies or am I giving in to having him become someone dying until he is dead? Will I know when the time is right?*

*B*y the end of April, Larry was changing rapidly. He couldn't speak at all. His gait was different. His legs were weak. I feared the worst. That was confirmed when we saw another specialist. It was my last option—a full muscular neurological test. The results confirmed that Larry had a form of ALS, which, when combined with Alzheimer's, meant the progression of his diseases would be quick. It was a rare finding. There was nothing more they could do.

I'll never forget that day, as Sarah, Eve, and I received the news with Larry sitting right by my side. It was the day I was no longer in charge. At least that's how it felt.

Was this bad news or good news? An odd question for sure. On the one hand, we would be losing Larry faster than we had ever expected. On the other hand, the thought of five or more years of watching Alzheimer's destroy him seemed intolerable.

None of us knew what to say, but the silence in the air called for something.

Eve began hesitantly, "I think we might be lucky." I was pretty sure her heart didn't believe that.

Sarah, thinking about all we had already experienced, added, "We will be spared the horrors."

I said, "Oh shit."

After the doctor left the exam room, my daughters and I sat there looking at Larry, each in our own thoughts. We were now faced with the news we feared most. There was silence as the room seemed to cave in around us.

In front of our eyes sat Larry, dressed as usual in his lawyer shirt and khaki pants, looking no different to us. Or was it my wishful thinking? Sure, he was thinner, his face was drawn, and at times he had a faraway look in his eyes, but he was always Larry to me.

There we sat, the four of us in this little exam room, waiting for what? No one prepared us. The door opened, and into this dreadful picture bounced a small woman, full of energy, with a warm and kind face. She could have been a loving relative. We were meeting our new palliative care doctor. As I said, we were not prepared or even expecting her.

She quickly introduced herself and then proceeded to give us the straight talk. Her words went right over our heads. In an attempt to be comforting, she said she would be by our side the whole way. I remember feeling nothing as she spoke. This was all new to us. We didn't even know what palliative care was. She made her exit, and the drama started to unfold at breathtaking speed.

Over the course of four hours, each member of her team entered the room and offered their expertise. First, we met a representative from the ALS Association, who had a handful of resource books for us. Next came a social worker asking if we needed assistance with care or even a recommendation for a facility, followed by a physical therapist who basically said Larry's abilities would be limited. Finally, we met a dietician who talked about healthy snacks. That was it. We had just met our palliative care team.

After all of this hustle and bustle, and four hours later, no treatment was advised. The combination of ALS and Alzheimer's presented too many challenges. We were to make Larry comfortable, understand he had limited bandwidth for physical activity, and maintain the best quality of his life we could.

And then we left to go home.

Just writing this now takes me back to our meeting five years earlier with the memory team, only this time we received some tenderness with the painful message. Still, we were left heartbroken. I know their job was to present the reality we faced, but in my mind, a pause in the action to simply say, "This must be very difficult for you to hear," might have felt like salve on our wounds.

Our minds were swirling as we tried to absorb the sobering information and the whirlwind experience we just had. Emotions were running very high. Typical of me, there was disbelief, only now it was combined with tremendous sadness. Once again, I had a harsh reality to accept. This was not a bump into reality; it was a full-blown crash.

But the drama was racing on.

It was just ten days after meeting the palliative care doctor when she called and said, "I think you should consider hospice."

I was beside myself. We had just learned about palliative care, and now we were moving to hospice. No way! This would truly mean the end. To say I struggled with the decision to accept hospice is an understatement. I felt it was completely giving up, something I fought off for five years.

As hard as I tried to fight against them at our first meeting, their argument was compelling. But I had to be convinced that hospice was more than a death sentence. The more I learned, the harder it was to argue with the prospect of additional services, supplies, drugs, adaptive equipment, and medical consultations, all covered by Medicare.

Yet that was "stuff." None of this took into account the frightening experience of dying.

My mind was filled with unanswered questions of how to proceed. *Would it require too much strength and stamina to continue the things that bring him satisfaction? Can he still bring in the paper every day? Would he be exhausted if we took a walk by the lake? Should he just sit in his place on the sofa?*

And then there was the underlying question: *Is hospice right for now?*

After much push and pull with the hospice team, I understood that my daughters and I would always be the decision-makers. Ultimately, I would have the final say. They made sure I knew that if things changed for the better, I could leave hospice at any time. I think that was to appease me because they knew he would not get better.

I made it very clear that my desire was to keep Larry at home.

Reluctantly, I signed the papers as my daughters looked on, skeptical of my commitment to it, yet trusting me. No resuscitation, no life-saving drugs, regular visits. It was a lot to take in.

The drama of that day ended with their final task. They handed me "The Box" that contained four drugs that are used at the very end of life. They were certain I would need it someday, but for now I was told to hide it away in a place where I could find it when it became important.

I had no interest in learning what these four drugs were, nor did I want any further details about how or why they would be used. Again, my avoidance of reality kept me protected. My daughters later told me they believed The Box contained death.

I took The Box and hid it as I was told. Then I cried and cried.

From that point things changed dramatically. Someone was constantly ringing the doorbell with a delivery of drugs, incontinence supplies, bed pads, sterile gloves, or whatever. If you watched this play out on stage, you would see Larry and me sitting in the middle and people coming at us from stage right, stage left, up the front aisles, and passing through to the other side.

Every fourteen days, a nurse and social workers needed to visit to adhere to Medicare requirements. This became a challenge since it was assumed I was always available when they requested time. When I asked that they work around my schedule, they accommodated, but it seemed unusual for them to have a patient take charge of setting appointments.

Throughout all of this chaos, Larry gave me glances that said, "What the heck is going on?"

The good news is that I had my therapist and Pauline at my side. Both were experienced with hospice care and end-of-life situations. My therapist wanted me to be prepared mentally as the end approached, while at the same time, she recognized my concerns about the hospice philosophy. She wanted to make sure I got the trained assistance I needed as Larry's body weakened so I could maintain my hard-fought role as Larry's wife.

Pauline believed, and wanted me to believe, that Larry wasn't as bad as they said. She and I were making adaptations to his needs constantly. Once again, I increased her hours. Astute to my heartache, she found time in the day to chat with me about things other than Larry. She even stayed overnight so I could go on retreat with the women I worked with. While clearly an employee, she was there for me whenever she could be. She read my grief.

When Larry had trouble getting up from the kitchen chair, she surprised me by having wheels put on a chair so Larry could move around or be pushed around. No wheelchair for Larry. Of course, if we needed to get one, hospice would have it at our door within hours.

Throughout the five years Larry and I lived through dementia, the pace of change, the immediacy of decisions, and the disruption of even the smallest day-to-day activities highlighted how ill-prepared I was to recognize "the right time" for anything, especially bringing hospice into our lives. *Was it an intrusion or a necessity? Was it too soon? How will I ever know?*

I could only ask questions that didn't give me clear answers, which meant all I could count on was what my heart was saying at a time when there weren't many options left.

In the end I had to trust that I was taking the right next steps at the right time.

No, Thank You!

Note to self: A while ago, Karen gave me a printed T-shirt with the words, "I don't tolerate incompetence." It was never truer.

In addition to hospice, I was informed that Larry was entitled to eighteen hours of free respite care from the ALS Association. The social worker encouraged me to accept this generous offer. All I could think of was another thing for me to schedule, another person for Larry to adjust to, and possibly more hassle than help. Nevertheless, I thought the offer was kind, and I agreed to it.

I was right. It was not a good decision.

I get irritated even thinking about this, so I'll make it short and pull out the only things I learned. First, my definition of respite was not what I received. Second, there was no time to put up with incompetence.

When I asked one of the ALS respite caregivers to make Larry lunch and then walked in the kitchen to find that she had heated an *entire* pound of sliced turkey (the good kind!) and stacked it between four slices of bread, I was mortified. Clearly, she didn't know how to make a sandwich, and I didn't have time to teach her. Between that and the fact that she seemed afraid of Larry, I had no trust in her ability to provide care. I had to ask her to leave my house. Good thing that was a day I sensed trouble and stayed close to home.

It didn't help that I felt sick and guilty when I left Larry with a person who didn't feel "right."

One of those respite attendants treated him like an invalid. My heart broke when I'd come home and find Larry in his chair, covered up to his neck with a blanket and his pants soaking. I didn't want to have to worry about his well-being when I was away. This service of respite became time lost with my husband. It was no gift.

After many occurrences like this, and, if you can believe it, even worse, I notified the ALS Association to let them know that I would no longer accept their help. To my satisfaction, this resulted in a long discussion with a wonderful woman who coordinated the respite program. I listened as she told me about their tremendous hardship in finding employees to meet their demands. She apologized profusely, and we engaged in a fruitful conversation. She was listening, and more importantly, believed me.

I told her I would like to see the job description of their respite helpers. For any employer, this would be a requirement. After a long pause, she admitted that they did not have one, so I volunteered to write one and send it to her.

After reviewing it, she thanked me and asked if she could make this part of their training materials. Without hesitation, I gladly agreed—anything if it would help them be of better service.

I've included a copy of that document. As I look at it again, I get upset just thinking about what would have been helpful and what I actually received. Maybe this will help those in need, as well as those attempting to serve that need.

What Is Respite?

- Time for self-care for the client's partner
- Peace of mind knowing their partner is with a competent and caring person
- Worry-free period away from the stress of daily life
- Knowing that the partner has been attended to with dignity and respect
- Minimal household chores done as directed

Job Description of an Aide Providing Respite Care

- Shows up on time, ready to work

- Provides care and safety for the client
- Provides compassionate and positive companionship for the client
- Treats the client as a person, not an invalid
- Talks to the client even if the client doesn't respond
- Monitors the client's eating so the client doesn't choke
- Makes simple meals as instructed
- Cleans up after meals
- Performs light household chores
- Anticipates what is needed and handles it
- Observes changes in the client's abilities, reports, and accommodates
- Maintains a balance of rest and activity for the client
- Handles toileting every two hours
- Assists in personal care and hygiene
- Assists in ambulation and mobility as needed
- Follows the list provided by the client's partner
- Communicates with the client's partner via phone or text as needed
- Brings nothing religious or spiritual into the house
- Acts quickly and responsively to emergencies
- Supervises with authority and compassion

Job Requirements

- Has approved training and licensing in health care, safety, and life-saving
- Has proven experience as a caregiver for persons with complications of dementia and ALS

- Has good personal hygiene
- Has a high school diploma or equivalent
- Is smart and a quick learner
- Is strong enough to lift and support a client
- Has ability to follow instructions and remember them when tasks are repeated
- Has good communication skills with English language proficiency
- Requires minimal instruction in order to perform simple housekeeping tasks
- Is able to prepare simple meals following guidelines for the client's diet
- Is unfazed by unpleasant tasks
- Keeps a professional demeanor at all times
- Is willing to go the extra mile

I Was Still in Charge

Note to therapist: *There are days I feel like I've lost control of everything. It's as if I'm a helpmate, or a witness to a process that keeps me from Larry.*

Her response: *Since you've never been much for compliance, it won't likely be satisfying to just agree to turn over a good deal of decision-making to a team of folks new to you. But there are still problems to solve, puzzles to work out, and decisions for you to make. They are some of the most important ones you will make in your life and in your marriage. These are not small things!*

*A*fter a few months with hospice, we had a disagreement. I was faced with the dilemma I feared would happen when I signed the papers for their services.

I'd been noticing for days that Larry was congested and coughing. He was lethargic and sleeping more than normal. One of the biggest worries at the end of life is pneumonia. With Larry's illnesses, this was even more of a threat.

Once again, Larry's change came on suddenly, which for me meant it was atypical of his diseases. I wanted to get him to the emergency room for assessment and, if needed, treatment. Knowing that my agreement with hospice was that they would be the first call for a medical issue, I followed the rule. But I knew that hospice would not administer any antibiotics or medications given the patient's life expectancy.

Within an hour, our nurse and social worker appeared. After a quick exam, I heard the familiar response, "It is just part of his disease progression." They didn't advise taking him to the ER.

"Of course," they said, "it's up to you."

But there was another rule; if I took him to the ER, I would have to leave hospice and then re-enlist if I wanted to return.

I was being tested. Out came those guiding principles.

My gut was saying, *I have to have a doctor see Larry.* He hadn't been to an internist for almost a year, which meant he hadn't had his meds checked nor any blood work done. Luckily, I kept his private insurance, so money wasn't an issue.

I sat on the sofa with Pauline, listening to the hospice nurse, while both of us knew we would take him to the ER, no matter the rules.

I looked at the social worker, who didn't say anything. Her eyes showed she was troubled, especially after I said, "I'm not going to just sit and let him be sick and do nothing about it."

In other words, right then, I didn't agree with the hospice philosophy of "let nature take its course."

To me that said, "Let him die."

Well, I wasn't ready for the end, and I didn't believe for a minute that Larry was either.

Reluctantly, they gave me the forms to fill out that would stop hospice services; I signed them easily. Then Pauline and I drove Larry to the nearest ER.

The lobby was packed. I'd forgotten how crowded ERs could be. I started to panic. *Did I make a mistake?*

I was so glad Pauline was with us. What if I had been alone? We sat for five hours. As it was getting later and later in the day, the staff started handing out blankets to keep all of us who were waiting from freezing from the air conditioner.

Finally, they called Larry's name. We were greeted by a kind and caring young doctor. It was as if Larry was his most important patient, even knowing there was a crowd just outside waiting to see him.

I felt myself breathing normally again. Someone was as concerned as I was about Larry's condition. He left nothing to chance: X-rays, ultrasound, blood work, the full package. Of course, this was another three hours, but I had no complaints. Someone was taking me seriously.

To a person, including nurses, doctors, and even the guy pushing the wheelchair, we received deep concern and understanding. There were actually words of comfort offered to me.

After all of this, they felt Larry had a respiratory virus that he would likely get over with rest and Tylenol.

All of that hassle for what? My peace of mind. I did what I felt was the right thing to do.

It wasn't difficult to sign up again for hospice. Getting the bill resolved between Medicare and my insurance company and then finally getting paid was another thing. It took almost a year to settle the account. No one could figure out what I had done and who was responsible. It was clearly an unusual situation.

On her subsequent visit, the social worker expressed her happiness that nothing was seriously wrong with Larry.

I said, "It was all worth it. I couldn't do nothing."

While she didn't realize it, her reply was revealing.

"Honestly," she said, "I think you did the right thing by taking him to the ER. If it was my father or husband, I would have done the same thing."

She had done her job by advising us not to go, but her heart told her something else.

I knew I needed the services of hospice, but this experience left me questioning.

Could I trust what the hospice team was advising? Were they just doing their job, following the hospice philosophy of reducing pain as terminally ill patients passed away? Was there any room for this social worker to be honest with me about her personal thoughts? Why did she tell me this after the fact? It's all complicated at a time when there doesn't seem to be a right or wrong answer.

Larry did recover from that virus. The nurses continued to show up, and the supplies and meds kept rolling in. But my relationship with hospice changed.

Then the quiet angel appeared.

There was no question that Larry's morning showers were getting harder and harder for both of us to keep up. Nevertheless, I was convinced that there was no need for hospice to provide a health aide to assist with hygiene.

I could do it! He was modest! It was our time!

They suggested I try a health aide one day a week. *OMG!* I loved that help.

Anita, the quiet angel, would get Larry all cleaned up and dressed for the day, and I would greet him, excited to be his wife, not his aide.

For over two years, my therapist had been trying to persuade stubborn me to bring in this type of help.

"You need someone like a valet so you can be a wife," she advised the first time I complained about helping Larry get ready in the morning. But I laughed and disregarded it. Then in a later session I whined about how I had to get Larry ready before me each morning, and she suggested the valet again, but I did nothing. It was a conversation that came up so many times that we started calling this imaginary valet David.

I kept saying, "I don't need a David in my house. This is sacred time, and I don't want anyone to steal it."

Well, as they say, timing is everything. I didn't have David; I had Anita. This angel taught me how to better assist Larry as his condition worsened. She ordered supplies and meds, always thinking about what I needed before I knew I needed it. I couldn't get enough of her.

She even showed up on Larry's last day on this earth to bathe him, ever so gently, calming both of us.

I learned many lessons about not allowing rules to keep me from doing what I believed was right and, at the same time, allowing myself to accept what I really needed. By doing so, I was able to look myself in the mirror and know I had kept my promise of doing everything I could for Larry, while at the same time savoring moments of just being with him. I had to learn to receive help, but I didn't have to give up. I was still in charge, and my heart was still guiding me even as time was growing short.

Hospice was not a curse. It was a blessing and even more so at the very end of Larry's life.

Hope Is a Process

Note to self: It's time to make peace with life as I know it. I'm not thinking about tomorrows as I did before.

And as I think about it now, given space to reflect, I have come to realize that a shift—one I didn't recognize at the time—happened in those last months with Larry. I was facing the end of Larry's life. Up until then, I had kept this crazy hope that I could do something to make it hurt less. One of my principles was even "Ground yourself in hope." But the acceptance that my five-year fight was coming to an end made that difficult to do.

C.R. Snyder, in his book *The Psychology of Hope*, describes hope as a way of thinking. Not an emotion, but a thought process. My process of hope had sustained me through the hardest and scariest of times. It gave me strength to maintain a mindset that kept me going and kept Larry going. Yet despair was inescapable, especially when watching Larry weaken before me and when others moved into our life offering "help" I needed but really didn't want.

All that was left was to be compassionate and turn to hoping for a peaceful end.

Hospice nurses continued their scheduled visits and were always kind and chatty. Sometimes, I wasn't sure what they were adding. But it met the one-hour visit requirement.

They kept offering me the hospice respite program where Larry could stay at a facility for two nights to give me a break. I don't think I need to explain how that fell on deaf ears. Leaving him in a strange place so I could get away was the opposite of what I wanted—I wanted more time with Larry, not less. I'm sure it is a great service for those in other situations, but not for me.

I turned down offers from hospice for reasons that made sense to me. Without them understanding what my heart was saying, they kept making suggestions. Finally, I had to face the fact that there were things hospice could offer that I was incapable of providing. But they never understood why I was slow to accept them. I had always hoped I wouldn't need them.

They offered to bring in a lift chair so Larry could get up more easily. I was certain I didn't need it.

"Not yet," I would say.

They suggested it again.

"Not yet."

I believed I could transfer him. When I finally yielded and allowed it to be delivered, it saved my body, and Larry could get up independently.

But accepting the lift chair was a big concession for me. It wasn't about the chair. It was about the chair putting distance between Larry and me. That was a heartbreaker that no one but me understood.

When our social worker came to visit me after Larry died, we chatted about many things. Along with appreciation, she got some "constructive feedback" from me.

"I know I resisted accepting the lift chair," I conceded.

She gave me the disapproving look that said, "Yes you did!"

"I don't think you understood that if we brought in that chair, he would be sitting off in a corner. I would lose the sweet moments of sitting next to him on the sofa and laying my head on his shoulder or holding his hand."

Her look told me this was an *aha* moment for her. "Oh my, I never thought of that!"

"I wasn't willing to give that up until I had no choice."

At the end of our conversation, she thanked me for providing her with "new insights."

It's instances like this that drove me to write this book. Someone needs to tell the story not only as it's lived but how it is felt for real couples.

Despite feeling like I gave in, Larry's lift chair made it easier for both of us.

The buttons controlling the lift motor gave him power—something in his control—and sometimes he used those controls to get our attention.

If we were in the room talking or watching something on TV, we would hear the motor starting as he began pushing the button, sending himself up and down repeatedly. He was entertaining us with his joyride—looking over at us, fully aware that he was being funny. When we encouraged him, his eyes would sparkle just a bit. Then he would keep going until we finally had to tell him to stop. Thankfully, my son-in-law recorded it one night. Watching that video now makes me smile with a tear. While providing many moments that became great memories, the chair demonstrated he still knew he could make us laugh.

With people around us all the time, there were things for me to do and nothing for me to do. My floors were swept, my waste baskets empty, Larry was content, and I was restless. I felt guilty not spending time with him and, it made no sense, but I missed doing my own laundry or washing the floor. Things were changing so quickly that I never felt settled into any pattern or routine for myself. I began to wonder if there was still anything to hope for.

The sad part of this was that it was becoming harder to find private moments with Larry, something that I wanted desperately. Even though our mealtimes were often just the two of us, they were somber. I'd talk to him, and he would just look at me. If we had time alone, I'd ask for hugs and kisses, or I'd give them to him unexpectedly. He tried to return the gesture, remaining a really good kisser.

And then there was the day that I couldn't have hoped for. We were alone in the morning. Larry was sitting at the kitchen table, where he reached for a nearby pen and pad of paper. The next thing I saw was him sitting in his formal lawyer position writing feverishly. Writing, writing, flipping the pages, and writing some more. He had lots to say. I let it go for almost half an hour, then came over to see what he had written. It was pages of gibberish interspersed with some almost recognizable words and rows of numbers. In some places it started as a legal document with numbered sequences.

Then there it was: *"I love you."*

I asked him if this was a letter for me. He nodded with his eyes. It was a beautiful moment, one I think of a lot. Things could have been so different had I seen things as hopeless and given up on him.

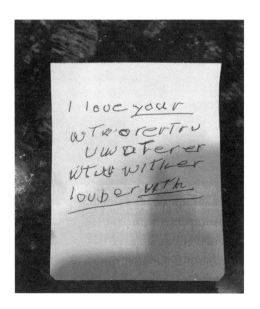

Till Death

Do Us

Part

One Last Time

Note to therapist: I often start a book, and if it gets hard or dull, I just skip to read the end. The Larry story is a hard one. I want to know the end, not create the end. The uncertainty of what each day will bring is difficult. Will this be a good day, a bad one, or the last one?

Her response: If you are looking at changes in Larry as signals of either (or both) his demise or your release—I don't think it's a good strategy.

"There are so many beautiful things in life," Rabbi Steve Leder writes, "that when they happen for the last time, we don't actually know that they are happening for the last time."

Rabbi Leder provides a stark reality and a good case for noticing life as it is lived, especially those scrapbook moments. None of us can be certain how much time we have ahead of us. We don't think about making "last times," unless, like me, I could see that Larry's time was running out.

I was losing Larry day by day. Over the five or more years of his illnesses, there had already been thousands of "last times." Each time Larry lost his ability to do one thing or another became a cause for grief. Each one like a small death. It was like water in a leaky bucket. It leaks little by little until it's dry.

As long as our bucket had water, I would make sure Larry had some important last times with things we held dear. These were my final hours to make sure that I would have no regrets.

What would Larry want? How will I feel in the end? The answers were not easy at this stage. I had to focus on making the most of our "last times" together.

We took our last family pontoon ride on Medicine Lake. We took the long drive to the cemetery in East St. Paul so he could stand by his parents' graves for the last time. Then as we always did afterward, Larry tasted his special corned beef and chopped liver sandwich at Cecil's Delicatessen located in the neighborhood where he grew up.

Whether a slow walk with the boys to our favorite spot on the lake for a picnic lunch, or a couple of holes at mini golf followed by a chocolate malt, we didn't stop.

And then there was our last family trip to the North Shore of Minnesota, something we had done in August for thirty years. It has always been a week for all of us to relax on the stunning shores of Lake Superior and one of those family traditions we all count on. Almost everything about the trip "up north," as Minnesotans say, was made up of things we did each and every year.

We have our favorite rest stops where we all meet on the drive up. We shop for pies at the same bakery and make our annual trip to the Ben Franklin store in Grand Marais to buy some overpriced souvenirs or T-shirts. We play the same games, climb rocks, and take the same hikes on the same trails. On the first night we eat clams and linguine, and on Friday we have a campfire Shabbat. As they say, it is tradition.

Could we do it one last time? I wasn't sure. Larry was failing fast.

A conversation with my family convinced me that the trip was on.

Sarah and Eve were insistent. "We will help make it happen. We promise."

That was when I realized they needed the last trip with Larry more than I did. They needed their final memories.

Weeks before the trip, I was overcome by the thought of this being Larry's last one with all of us. I wanted to make it memorable.

Through our thirty years of family trips to the North Shore, I collected hundreds of photos. I thought it would be fun to make a slideshow that we could all watch when we were sitting together by the fire in our log home. Did I really think it would be fun, or was I writing part of Larry's eulogy?

I had Larry help me go through the photos. It was something we could do together. We sat on the sofa and went through years of photos. While I would talk about this or that, he would listen. Then he'd move a picture from one pile to the other. With one or two photos, he would hold them and stare at them, then show them to me, as if he had some prominent memory.

The final selection of photos included images of great times. But I had a hidden agenda. The photos I selected for the slideshow were mostly photos of Larry interacting with his daughters, his sons-in-law, his grandsons, and of course me. There were funny photos and touching photos. He was hugging us, doing puzzles, skimming rocks with Sam, and sitting by the fire with us. All sweet memories we could hold for another moment. And since they went back in time, there were many photos of Larry when he was healthy and strong, and photos of me when I was young and thin.

I worked hard on the project, but when we left for the trip, it wasn't finished. It still needed background music and some tweaking. I wanted a stellar production.

Lawrence drove as Larry and I rode in the back. On the drive, I mentioned to Eve that I needed music appropriate for the show. That became our task on the five-hour drive. She searched iTunes and found songs that fit the mood. She suggested tunes about memories, togetherness, happy times, adventures, and the one I used to end the slideshow, "Time in a Bottle."

It was like coming home when we arrived at the big log house we had rented for the past five years. Then we moved in. When I say "moved in," you'd think we were staying for months with all of the gear, groceries, books, games, and what seemed like hundreds of shoes—nine people in one house and Larry in the middle of it all, as always. Only this time he watched quietly.

From the very beginning, I could see that this was going to be a very difficult trip, but in the end, I'm so grateful that we all pushed to make it happen.

Most of the first day, I worked to finish the slideshow. It was all I could think of. I was excited to show it to the family, but I was also nervous. I wanted it to be special for everyone, knowing it wasn't going to be easy to watch.

On our second night, we sat together in front of the big TV screen. It was time for my big show.

With tissues in hand, I sat behind everyone. I wanted to watch them.

As we saw the years go by, one person or the other would make a remark. They laughed at old hairstyles, their weight, and the favorite clothes they were reminded of.

I'd hear, "Oh, I still have that shirt."

"That was a good puzzle."

Max saw his hair go from brown to pink to green, then blue, and Nate went from short hair to long flowing hair.

And Sarah saw a reminder of her short hair after cancer treatment.

I heard, "Oh, I remember that time," or, "Look at you."

Each time a photo of Larry came up, I could feel the emotion change in the room. There they were, captured in a photo with their dad, and their Papa once again alive and full of energy, a loving parent who always made sure that they were having a good time.

I heard a sweet "ohhh" when they saw a photo of Larry starting the campfire. It was his job, because after all, he was a Boy Scout. A soft sigh when they saw Larry holding a little boy's hand as they climbed the rocks on the shore with the mist in the air around them.

There were photos of the girls when they were young as Larry helped them hike the trails. As Aaron and Lawrence joined the family, photos showed them just kibitzing with Larry.

Max actually reacted with a smile when he saw Larry wrestling with him on the bed.

Sam commented on his ability to skim rocks as he saw a photo of Papa and him at the shore.

And there were always bubbles in the photos, giant ones that Nate would blow and Larry would pop.

And no memory of the North Shore would be complete without a photo of Larry sitting quietly in the corner absorbed in a good book.

Photos of me were always the ones I had to ask someone to take, so they were mostly of me sitting on a bench with the family around me. Everyone had their moments. There were multiple photos of our family taken just before we were ready to leave for home. It was part of the tradition. Everyone knew it marked the end of the trip, even though we were already planning for next year.

As the slideshow played, I watched Larry more than the screen. I could see his eyes tear up at times. The closest I got to knowing what he was thinking was when a photo of him with a grandson or daughter came on the screen. He would look over at them as if to say, "That's us." As the show ended with Jim Croce singing the words, *"If I could save time in a bottle,"* I couldn't talk.

Everyone in that space knew that this trip to the North Shore was to be savored because it would be Larry's last, and our loss.

It was a hard trip for me physically. My knee was swelling from schlepping Larry for months, and it was difficult to walk. The kids saw how exhausting my life was, but they couldn't help with things that needed to be private between Larry and me.

Trying to keep things somewhat normal, the family went out of their way to include Larry as much as possible. Sadly, there simply were things we couldn't do any longer.

But oh, how we tried.

Even if it was playing cards with him when what he was doing made no sense at all or sitting with him in the sun watching as I played mini golf with the boys, he was with us.

Our last night was a Friday. That meant we would have our campfire Shabbat on the rocks by the shores of Lake Superior. We would light our candles and say our prayers as the sun was setting and the waves were crashing. It was a tradition that held so much meaning and years of memories.

My sweet grandsons helped me get Larry down the steep stairs of the house, over the rocks to the shore, and into a chair. The fire was glowing, and the hot dogs were ready to be roasted. I took one look at Larry and saw him shivering from a chill. We tried to cover him with jackets, but he couldn't stop shaking. Reluctantly, I took him back to the house.

The two of us sat inside watching the activities on the shore from the window. After a while Eve came up to the house and brought hot dogs, charred just the way Larry liked them. He quickly ate his and then mine too. For Larry, there was nothing like a kosher hot dog cooked over the fire.

I was feeling bad that I couldn't be near the fire. Eve could tell and offered to relieve me, sending me down to the rocks.

I was busy making s'mores when I looked up and saw Larry coming down those steep steps by himself. Eve had turned her back, and Larry, determined to join us on the rocks, was out the door. Luckily my grandson ran up to assist and brought him to us safely. He wasn't going to miss out on anything—and he didn't.

The photos and stories of memories from our last trip together at the North Shore are bittersweet.

The decision to make this last journey a trip filled with tradition supported everything I believed in for five years. What if we didn't have this time together? What if I hadn't maintained the mindset of keeping him going, keeping him where the action was? This was one of those decisions where reward won over risk. As long as Larry was with us, we would continue to make treasured memories, even if they were for the last time.

Goodbye,
My Beloved

Note to self: I was napping upstairs while Larry was with Pauline. When I woke, I was totally overwhelmed from the dream I just had. Larry talked to me! It's not like anything that has ever happened before, and I don't know how to think about it. He said clearly, "BELIEVE." It really shook me and I can't figure out what it meant. I've gone from "believe" Larry will get better, which was impossible, to "believe" that what is meant to be will be. Now I think I need to "believe" I will survive?

When we returned from the North Shore, it quickly became clear that Larry was at the end of his life. Our home was changing as well, as if the lighting was dimming, and ordinary things were disappearing little by little, while foreign objects were appearing.

September is our Jewish High Holidays. Larry and I never missed a service at the temple in all of our years together. On Rosh Hashanah, we would dress in our nicest outfits, fill a row in the sanctuary with family, and chant the familiar prayers. When services ended, we would return home to taste the round sweet challah bread symbolizing a wish for a "sweet year." Yom Kippur, the Day of Atonement, followed ten days later. After fasting and spending a full day in the synagogue asking for forgiveness and praying to be entered in the Book of Life for another year, services would end at sundown with the blowing of the shofar, a ram's horn. It's a soulful sound that cries for hope. Each year as we exited the temple, Larry and I would embrace in a loving hug wishing each other a healthy and happy New Year, then turn to the family and do the same.

That didn't happen.

I thought long and hard about what to do about services. One day, Larry was going with me; another day, he wasn't. I couldn't bear to think about going alone. Then I started thinking of all the "what ifs." I had to admit, it would be too much for both of us.

Hard as it was to face letting go of a tradition, I knew it was necessary. I decided to go to services alone for the first time in over fifty years. But the holiday was still special. It would likely be the last of Larry's High Holy Days.

As I got ready to attend the temple for Rosh Hashanah, Pauline helped Larry get into his good trousers and suit jacket. I needed to see him as I always did on this important day. He was acting pretty cocky as he walked around in his dress loafers, clicking his heels on our wooden floor. Larry knew it wasn't an ordinary day. Pauline took a photo of the two of us, our last one together. Then I left for the temple alone to join Eve and Lawrence.

Not having him sit by my side during services made me uneasy. I had trouble focusing on the words I was reading, and my silent prayers brought me to tears. I honestly didn't know what to pray for.

It was unbelievable that in the sanctuary, where every seat was always filled with congregants, there was an empty seat next to me.

Dark days came fast. My sister and brother-in-law came to town for what they soon figured out would be their last visit with Larry. They were shocked at how he had weakened.

I worked very hard to keep it together while they were here. I still couldn't allow myself to appear pathetic. But on Sunday, a day before they left, I lost it. Larry was dying, and in a way, so was I.

Sarah could tell that I was having a hard time and called the family together, including Pauline. Sarah and Eve sat me down and made me face the fact that I needed twelve hours of help every day.

"We need to keep you alive," Sarah said with force.

I knew it, but it was hard to accept someone in my house all the time. But if I was going to keep Larry at home, I had no choice.

We hired another wonderful caring aide, Selina, to give Pauline some days off. It was at this point that I felt like I lost control. In many ways, I did.

Pauline and Selina were knowingly preparing me for what was ahead.

I will admit that I was upset when one of them said, "He is ours now."

I challenged this vehemently. However, that woke me up. He was not theirs. He was my husband. I was his wife. I needed to be with him as much as possible, even if our privacy was limited.

That drove me to find moments, minutes, and a few times, an hour to be close to each other. These women saw the signs and moved to another room to fold clothes or do whatever so we could be left alone. There is no question; this was a difficult time, but I continued to hang on to the very last minute.

How did I want to feel in the end that was coming quickly?

I watched as my dear Larry needed more and more help. The look in his eyes let me know he hated this life. When I had to order adult bibs from Amazon, I cried, but not as hard as when I saw him wearing one and Selina feeding him.

Larry's big brown eyes were dull that day.

In October, hospice pushed for me to get Larry into a facility. No surprise, I refused. There were those guiding principles again. But the stairs were now a big obstacle. The only showers in the house were upstairs or on the lower level.

Our lovely health aide, Anita, came to my rescue. She looked at my lower level and said, "He could be down here. We can bring in a hospital bed. You have a shower and a big TV."

She reminded me that hospice would provide all the equipment I needed. It could have everything a facility would have, and I'd still be with him. *Ahh, a plan to keep Larry home!* I kicked into gear, and so did Eve and Lawrence.

We cleaned the downstairs and moved furniture to make room for a hospital bed. I even asked the hospice to bring in another lift chair, still believing there could be times when Larry was able to be upstairs in the family room and he would need a chair there. Preparing the space gave us something to do at a time we felt helpless.

All along, I knew he would never get down there. Larry wouldn't want it. I was just going through the motions.

The Wednesday before Larry died, my therapist and I had an emotional session. Our fight together to save the essence of Larry had nearly come to an end. With her most caring professional guidance, she helped me face the inevitable.

It was a devastating moment when she said, "Myrna, where is The Box?"

"The Box?" I didn't know what she was referring to.

"Yes, the box of drugs the hospice gave to you at the first meeting."

I forgot about it until that moment.

She has since told me that I looked at her as if I was hearing a foreign language.

Wanting me to take action, she pressed, "You need to leave now and call hospice and your girls. It is time to plan for the final hours."

She had been preparing me for this since our first meeting. I was as ready as I could be.

Later that day, I called a family meeting with the hospice team and asked Pauline to sit with us. Just like we did five years earlier when we were absorbing Larry's diagnosis, we were all seated in a circle in the living room, only this time we were planning his final days.

While we were talking, the doorbell rang. It was the delivery guys bringing the hospital bed, a wheelchair, and much more to be set up downstairs for Larry. I just sat there and let it all happen, knowing in my heart that Larry would never see the downstairs, nor did I want it to end that way for him.

I was in the meeting, but not.

All of a sudden, I realized that Larry was sitting watching this meeting from the kitchen table. There we were, all talking about him, which, as I've said, he disliked immensely. When I turned to look at him, he looked at me, and I could see he was upset.

I asked, "Would you like to join us?"

Knowing his answer, I moved him next to me. He needed to be with us in the circle. We were all talking about his fate. From all those lessons that I had learned over the past years and the principles that guided me, I knew that it was important for Larry to be part of his end-of-life conversation.

That same night, Larry gave up. He wasn't going to live his life as it was.

About two in the morning, he took a turn. I crawled into his bed, hugging him close, wishing he would die in my arms.

Selina came early the next day, and we both knew that the time had come. The hospital bed was moved from the downstairs to the bedroom and Larry was made comfortable in it. There was no fight left in him.

Believe it or not, hospice gave me one last fight. They strongly recommended that I get Larry into a hospice facility quickly. They even said I would regret not doing this.

My response came out strong. "Larry built this house, he raised his family in this house, and he will die in this house."

There was nothing more to be said.

My therapist made sure I could live with this decision. "Think about how you will feel knowing that Larry has passed in the room you will sleep in after he is gone."

There was no question in my mind that this was what we both wanted.

All day Thursday, the girls and I were by Larry's side as he faded away in front of our eyes.

That night, Sarah and Eve crawled into bed with me. We comforted each other with Larry in his hospital bed in front of us. Pauline snapped a photo of the three of us, which I now have framed and set on my dresser—Mom and her loving daughters.

On Friday, I hardly left him. The hospice nurse was on the scene, but I have little recollection of what she did or how The Box was used. I left that to Sarah.

Selina kept watching me and then made room in the bed so I could lie with Larry for a short while. I was by his side as I promised.

All the nurses were shocked at how fast things went. I knew that this was what Larry wanted. We needed to make this as peaceful as possible for him and for us.

Amidst all of this, I felt the need to call our rabbi and let her know what was happening. It was odd because the thought of needing spiritual guidance hadn't even crossed my mind until it became strong and urgent.

Within hours she was sitting with our family.

"Tell him you will be OK and that he can go in peace," she advised us.

While true, these words were hard to say, but we did, over and over.

Later the temple cantor brought his comforting voice to bless Larry with traditional prayers.

There was a lot of activity in our house during the last forty-eight hours of Larry's life, but each one of us got to say goodbye.

Even after all I had endured, I was numb and in disbelief that this was the end.

As the sun set, all of us gathered around him—just as we always did at five thirty on Friday. Larry took his last breath. He died as he lived. No fuss, no drama. He was ready.

It was the end of a wonderful life and a loving story.

No Regrets!

Note to self: While I'm filled with sadness, I have so much to be grateful for. I can honestly say I did my best for Larry, and I am alive.

Soon after Larry died, I replayed the last days of our life together in my head. I was making hard decisions with certainty like never before, believing that I was guided by a divine force. Sometimes I was so certain of what to do that it amazed me. Other times I didn't care what happened because in my mind it made no difference. *This drug or that one? Windows open or shut? Music or no music? Should his brother come or not?* I was laser focused on what mattered most to me—letting Larry know I would be OK, that I loved him, and our life together had meaning. In those last hours, "What would Larry want?" became "What would we both want?"

Others may have thought they were directing traffic to ease my load. They may have eased it, or they may have at times added to it, but in hindsight, I know I was ultimately in charge the entire time.

Thinking about it now, I've come to understand that it wasn't a divine force at all. It was my own strength, built with hard work in order to live by a loving commitment. I didn't always get it right, but I really tried!

For over five years, I was guided by principles and a mindset of what can be, instead of focusing on what I was losing. But most importantly, I was driven by love for a man who had always been by my side, as I was for him. We were a team. I wasn't going to let him down.

He would have approved.

In the end, my family is closer than ever. I maintained the loving relationship with them that could have so easily been ignored. And while feeling tremendous sorrow, I kept myself alive. I am strong enough to face my future.

Larry is still with me, by my side, but now he is a photo, a collection of scrapbook moments, a lawyer shirt, a place at the table, a recorded voice, and a ring around my finger. He is a tear and a smile. He is the soft gray shirt that hangs in the closet. It's the one he wore when we had our last dance together. When I see it, I remember swaying to the music.

This was the hardest role I have ever played. There were moments when I wasn't sure I could do it. There were disappointments and setbacks. And for sure there were tears—lots of them.

My well-known lack of patience was tested. I was forced to be vulnerable.

Today I am more sentimental, more empathetic, and more forgiving. I learned when to trust others and when to trust myself. And I found the gift of therapy and allowed myself to receive it. Most importantly, I felt the power of unending love.

As a result of my role as Larry's wife through all these difficult years, I can say that my life had meaning and purpose. Every day, I was challenged to stare down fear. Giving in was not an option. It's no wonder I experienced exhaustion for months after Larry died.

Despite the heavy load I carried, I believe that things could have ended differently. There would be no story to tell here if I had not maintained the mindset of lovingly losing my life partner and then building a strategy for living through dementia.

I didn't resent my exhaustion because it was energy put to the right purpose. I can't imagine how much more I would have lost had I not held on so tight and persevered. Larry was treated with love, honor, and dignity. He deserved nothing less.

Engraved on his tombstone are the words that describe him so well—*A Good and Beloved Man.*

And most importantly, he was with me to the end, even to the last dance.

How do I feel in the end? No regrets!

If grief is equated to love, I accept it.

Looking Back

*A*s we approached the first anniversary of Larry's death, my daughters and I were sipping tea around the dining room table when a memorable conversation happened spontaneously. It reveals a lot about a family living through dementia.

It was also days after Yom Kippur, which includes a tradition of apologizing to anyone we may have hurt over the past year and forgiving those who may have hurt us. This timing opened the space for a deep and reflective conversation that was candid, revealing, and forgiving. My daughters validated some of my thinking and also gave me another perspective—theirs. I realized that I wasn't perfect, but neither were they.

Our conversation started with me sharing something that was at the forefront of my mind.

"I realized yesterday that it is easier to ask for help now that Dad is gone than in the past five years. Why is that?"

Eve began, "In those first months, and even first year, I felt you had forgotten that we were adults."

In agreement, Sarah added, "We could see that you were embarrassed by Dad's failings and the adjustments you had to make. You were always trying to cover them up and keep them hidden from the family."

They were correct. I worked very hard to protect them from anything ugly. I was made of super strength, after all. I wasn't going to look pathetic to my daughters. Nor was their dad going to lose his dignity in their eyes. I believed it was my burden, not theirs.

"We didn't need protection," Sarah said.

Together we talked about the old habits we had to break. Habits like me learning to *ask* instead of *tell* and then drop the tone of voice I was known for when I was disappointed in them.

"It made us feel unappreciated," Sarah said.

Eve looked at me, a bit timidly. "It took a while before you realized that as adults, we had the right to say 'no' if there were things we weren't able to handle."

In my mind, I was thinking, *But I asked for help.*

Eve continued, adding a dose of compassion, "You did learn after a while and started accepting this without demonstrating disappointment or getting upset."

I was pleased that they actually gave me praise for learning and improving.

To their credit, they admitted that it took some time for them to realize how my load was different from theirs. Once they took a serious look at how my marriage had changed, how my life had changed, and how I had changed, they made an effort to turn from their old reactions of fighting me to providing empathy and an understanding ear. I thanked them for this realization.

When I told them how I hated to give a daily weather report about the climate in the house or to go down the path of "You'll never believe what Dad did today," for fear of sounding like a whiner, I received a sober, loving response.

"Mom, that was part of your daily grind. You needed to be real. It was you talking about your day, just like we report on ours."

"When you got honest about things, we knew when we could offer assistance, rather than wait to be asked or be expected to read your mind."

Wow!

And then, both of them opened up about Larry's incontinence. They admitted that they had concerns about handling something so private with their dad. Yet we all knew that they couldn't give me time away without addressing Larry's toileting needs.

Sarah admitted, "I did things I never thought I could. I'd surprise myself in how level-headed I could be even though I didn't like what I saw. In the moments when my natural reaction was to be totally irritated, what came out of my mouth was only respect to him as my father and an adult."

Then Eve retold an experience where Larry had an accident with her. "I didn't tell you because I didn't want you to be upset. I just wanted you to learn to trust me and let me choose which responsibilities I was or was not willing to take."

Interesting that she was protecting me. Yes, my daughters were adults.

As we sat with a box of tissue in the middle of the table and our hands wrapped around our teacups, we entered a difficult subject, but one we couldn't leave out of our reflections of the past years. The time when Larry was struck with GBS was agonizing for all of us. As I wrote in an earlier chapter, it was a time when Larry was temporarily paralyzed and hospitalized for twenty-two days. At that time, all I could think about was how my whole world was going to change. In my mind, he would never recover, and my life would never be the same. I was feeling very sorry for myself as I watched the sequence of events unfold.

"I could never have gotten through the long ordeal without both of you by my side," I told them, as I had done so many times.

I will never be able to express enough gratitude for the amazing things they did during that time. They were Larry's champions, encouraging him to work hard at his physical therapy and trying to cheer him. Eve came to the hospital on her lunch break or after work to sit with him, so I could get some rest. Once he got home, she took Family Medical Leave (FMLA) using four unpaid hours a week to be with Larry so I could keep working.

But until this Yom Kippur conversation, I hadn't realized the degree of angst they were experiencing as Larry
was stricken with this horrible illness. Like me, they got
scared. None of us knew if he would recover from GBS.

Eve recalled her heartsick feelings as she said, "This
was an awakening. I started thinking that this was what
the future might look like."

Visibly upset, even years later, Sarah hesitantly told
me how one day in his hospital room she saw her dad
naked. "That's nothing I ever wanted to see." Then as if
taken back to that time, she continued, "Suddenly I was
aware of the indignity he was facing."

As I write what I heard from them and their emotional
experience, I am hopeful that I apologized for my lack of
compassion at a time when our future seemed so bleak.

This intense conversation ended with us talking about
their husbands' roles as the family dealt with Larry's dementia. My two sons-in-law were definitely in the picture, but not as visible. Yes, they provided hugs and comforting words. They would try to help by coming over
for an hour or two to allow me to run out. But Sarah
pointed out to me something she didn't think I trusted.

"I don't think you really understood that they were
holding up their wives during this time. Dad's illness had
a ripple effect on my household, my marriage, and our
sons. Aaron kept the waters calm at home."

As we sat together, I listened intently. I was moved
by what we remembered, separately and together. But
more importantly, I was comforted by the appreciation
we gave each other for how we handled complicated and
unimaginable situations.

I'm glad I realized early that everyone would have their own unique relationship with Larry right up to the end. Those relationships required time and nourishment so they could capture their own scrapbook moments. I will always remember my two girls sitting on the sofa writing the eulogy they delivered so beautifully at Larry's funeral. They sat inches away from each other, giggling and crying. What they wrote was a tribute to a good man and a great father. As Eve said at the end of her remarks, "He taught us how to live, and he taught us how to die."

After Larry died, our family began to re-establish old patterns and create new ones. The good news is that together, Larry and I built a great foundation to stand on. We assured Larry in his last hours that we would all be OK, that he gave us a beautiful life, that we would live on with him in our memory, and that he could leave us knowing his life was a blessing to his family. Truer words were never spoken.

Our family dynamics are different today. We are grieving in our own way, with a deeper appreciation of our family's loving relationships. I hear understanding conversations. I don't hear judgment. I hear expressions of feelings and emotions. I see more hugs. And we are starting to have crazy laughter again. As our conversations—still around our dining room table—continue each Friday night, I find myself quieter. Now I sit in Larry's spot at the head of the table. I gaze at my adult children and at my grandsons who have grown to be tall young men, and I watch their interplay with great pride, thinking *Larry would have loved being here.*

Epilogue

I am now alone. I'm no longer a wife.

And just like I avoided the title of caregiver, I won't accept being called a widow.

Whenever I hear "widow," I see an image of a woman shrouded in black, her face covered in a black veil, wearing black gloves, dabbing away tears in her eyes with a white lace hanky. All around her is darkness. That is not me.

But who am I?

One of my goals for the five years I just wrote about was to survive—to preserve my own identity. In many ways, I did a pretty good job of that. What I didn't anticipate was how my identity would change, how my internal and external selves would shift, and what it would be like to figure out who I am and who I want to be. I'm still working on that. This epilogue is not really an end of the story. It is an end of a chapter of my life and the end of a loving marriage.

Larry died on Friday, November 1, 2019. It was as if a light switch had been flipped, and once again my life changed.

In accordance with Jewish customs, Larry's funeral and burial took place three days after he passed. Pauline took charge of clearing the house of anything related to Larry's illness and put everything back to normal. Five years of sickness had disappeared. Family and friends came and went, leaving behind enough food for months to come.

Then the circus ended. The house was silent. It was me and memories, both good and bad ones. Larry's drawers and closet were filled with lifeless clothes, and I now had four bathrooms and four TVs to myself. I believed I would be all right. It was one of my Superwoman fantasies.

And then one month after Larry died, I started writing. At first it was like a release of the toxins, a purge of hardships, and lots of soggy tissues. As I wrote, and with each of the many drafts and edits, I relived episodes and emotions over and over. I couldn't leave Larry behind, and truthfully, I didn't want to.

For three months, I floated through life, doing all the things that needed to happen after a death in the family. I immediately returned to my work with women and changed a few things around the house. I thought I was doing well going through the grief process as I had come to understand it.

Then in early March, COVID-19 hit—a pandemic bringing lockdown and isolation. Like so many around the world, life changed, as everyone was overtaken by uncertainties and unknowns. I couldn't feel sorry for myself knowing that people were dying without being able to say goodbye.

For fourteen months, I sat in my house, not just alone because Larry was gone, but alone and with no place to go. I didn't even feel the cold of our Minnesota winter because I hardly ever went out. COVID gave me an excuse to sit and write. I had something to do—something with meaning. I had a purpose. Yet in my heart, I knew that writing kept me in a state of remembering instead of a state of living.

I was grieving in a bubble.

The vaccine freed me. Little by little, I cautiously stepped a toe, then both feet, into a new life of whatever "normal" was to become for me. My mask tentatively came off—a good metaphor for emerging from the security of my home. I could no longer hide behind the mask and not think about what was next.

It took another conversation in the mirror.

Myrna, whatever normal is going to be for you without Larry, it's time to figure out how to live in it.

The question no longer is, "What would Larry want?"

It has become, "What does Myrna want?"

I'm learning that this question can't be answered easily. I won't find the answer without living in the question for as long as it takes.

One day, I woke up and felt different. I went to the cemetery and told Larry he would always and forever be with me, and now I needed to create a new story for myself. I knew he would agree.

Then I bravely told my therapist that I was ready to leave her and go my own way. I said tearfully, "I know you will always be there for me, but I need to move on."

And then to my disbelief, my grieving process took hold in a way that shook me. I heard someone say as the first COVID restrictions were ending, "It's time to start doing all the things you stopped doing."

That wasn't the case for me.

As I started reentering and reexperiencing life, I got smacked in the face with old memories, huge realizations, and things I stopped doing and couldn't do again.

Walking by the Macy's men's department and seeing the piles of jeans made my heart stop. Going to an acupuncture appointment and walking down the hall past the men's room sent me into an emotional tilt. Being with friends, who all had husbands in their lives, made me uncomfortable and withdrawn. And when I got an announcement that the Rocky Mountain train trip was running again, I was forlorn. Even if I could do it now, I wouldn't.

People say the first Thanksgiving, the first Passover, the first anniversary without your loved one is always the hardest. But my first holidays were on Zoom. They weren't normal. How would the upcoming holidays feel without Larry at the head of the table?

I found myself having lots of ordinary moments when I'd suddenly miss Larry and wish he were near me. I'm glad that I understood it was all part of a process of grief described by experts I follow. Rabbi Leder describes grief as waves of all magnitudes, sometimes overtaking you when you least expect it. David Kessler talks about the sixth stage of grief as "meaning," which allows you to find a path forward.

My path was anything but clear.

And then I had a roller-coaster week that left me with a stark and emotional realization: I was a single woman.

The week started on a high note, with my first post-COVID party with friends, all vaccinated and without masks. I never hugged women like that before. Together we celebrated life anew. Then Becky, who had lost her husband a year before me, talked about her upcoming trip to Australia.

"Why don't you come with me?" she encouraged.

The first thing out of my mouth was, "I can't."

"Why not?" she asked, and then told me about many of the trip's highlights.

I was quiet, thinking to myself, *Why not?* I was alone and could do anything I wanted. It was an *aha* moment. "Let me think about it, Becky."

The next day, Nancy asked me to go to an art gallery event with her.

"My husband and I will pick you up."

At first, I wanted to decline. An event without Larry? Being picked up like a third wheel? But I yielded to her offer and enjoyed myself more than I expected.

Then when Sarah and Aaron informed me that they had purchased a new home, I was sent into irrational thinking. They found a house they loved and would no longer be five minutes from me. The news hit me hard, which might seem crazy. They wouldn't be that far away, and Eve and Lawrence were still nearby. My friends had children in other states! But I couldn't sleep that night. It felt like another loss. The boys wouldn't be able to ride their bikes and just drop in. They would be leaving a house that held years of emotional family history. But Sarah and Aaron were adults making their own decisions about their future. They didn't need my approval.

I still am, and hopefully always will be, the beloved matriarch, but now I'm playing less of a role in their lives. The boys have grown into fine young men with minds of their own. I know I'm not as entertaining for them anymore.

Sometimes I find myself just watching my beautiful family as they interact. I watch as if I'm not there, seeing their life unfold without me. It's all good and gratifying, yet it's still unsettling. It's new territory for me.

I was struggling to find my way.

It was one of our Friday night family dinners that got me back on track. We were all sitting around the dining room table toasting Sarah and Aaron's home purchase. Sarah could tell I was a bit fragile.

"This is a big change," she started. "We went through so much in the last few years, and living this close to you really made it easier to provide the support we needed to give each other. I'm sad"—she paused—"and scared"—she paused again—"but also excited. You taught me that change can be a very good thing, and it's time."

That opened the floodgates as I poured out my fears to my loving family. "COVID put a detour in my grief," I told them. I didn't have to explain much; they understood.

Then I said, "It's up to me to figure out how to get to my last dance."

Eve looked aghast at this statement. I was pretty shocked by my own words too.

Then Aaron said emphatically, "No! You need to keep dancing."

Sarah followed with, "This needs to be the epilogue for your book and the beginning of your next."

They were right.

It is time to start to dream again, only this time it is about me—the things that I enjoy, the new adventures I can find, and getting my health back. I want to age gracefully, stay relevant, and have meaning in my life as I live and leave a great legacy for my family and for the world.

My mirror would say to me, *It is time to think about yourself now. You know what to do. So do it!*

Acknowledgments

I discovered a lot about gratitude over the past years, and even more after writing this story.

As weird as it might sound, it's because of the COVID restrictions that this book was completed. I had no place to go and a lot on my mind. I'm not grateful for the pandemic at all—in fact, there were moments during the early days when I thought the world was changing in such a way that my words would have no relevance—but I kept going.

It goes without saying that the value of this book was enhanced by the contributions provided by my therapist as I lived the story and we did amazing work together.

She reviewed many drafts and helped me make salient points with a professional eye.

Thanks to my best friend Karen Stinson for reading several of my worst drafts and still telling me they were great.

My daughter Eve Raymond tried to edit my early drafts but knew I had a long way to go. I'm so grateful she encouraged me to stick with it and in the end helped me make the final edits that tied things in a bow. And thanks to her husband Lawrence, who provided little reminders of things I had forgotten.

Thank you to my daughter Sarah Kesher for providing reality checks when I needed them and helping me synthesize my thinking when my brain felt mushy; and to Aaron Kesher, the grammarian in the family, who tried to help me understand how to use commas. Sorry, Aaron.

Thanks to Stuart and Joann Marofsky, who asked me every week how the book was coming and if I included great things about them in it—and I did.

I'm forever grateful to my loving and supportive sister, Lenore Kelner, who commiserated with me when things got hard as I lived the story and as I wrote this book. And to her husband Paul, who "checked in" to see how I was doing.

To the many (and I mean many) women in my life who took an interest in this book, always asking about my progress and then cheering me to the end. I'm beyond grateful.

I'm not sure how the book would have been completed without the skillful review of Bonnie Mueller. Not only did she get me to the end, but more importantly, she provided cheerful and uplifting comments, even while wiping tears from her eyes.

Thank you, Amy Quale, of Wise Ink, for saying, "You need to call yourself an author now." And to her skilled team, including Emily Krempholtz, Patrick Maloney, Abbie Phelps, and Hannah Kjeldbjerg, who had the patience I was lacking.

How fortunate I was to be introduced to Suyao Tian, the gifted artist whose beautiful cover design adds elegance to the story.

I'm also grateful for the professionals I've cited in the book who realize that dementia must be seen through the lens of living. I only hope this community grows as more and more hear the stories from those who are willing to tell them.

Thank you to those partners currently living through dementia or a chronic illness with a loved one, who read and commented on the book.

Finally, I'm grateful to my beloved husband, Larry Marofsky, who gave me a story to tell.

About the Author

Myrna Marofsky is an entrepreneur and consultant, mother, and grandmother. After she'd previously written two business books, it was her husband's dementia diagnosis that led her down a new path that resulted in this memoir. After years of facilitating groups of women business owners, she has mastered the art of asking questions that uncover new ways of thinking, a skill she benefited from when forced to redefine her life and the term "caregiving."

Where to Go Next

Visit www.myrnamarofsky.com to request author appearances, buy additional copies of *To the Last Dance*, and receive discounts for bulk purchases.

A portion of book sales will be donated to Second Harvest Heartland®, where the author's husband, Larry, was a volunteer for two years during the course of his dementia.

Second Harvest Heartland® is a Minnesota-based nonprofit working to end hunger through community partnerships. For more information, visit www.2harvest.org.